WBCA's Defensive Basketball Drills

Women's Basketball Coaches Association

Library of Congress Cataloging-in-Publication Data

WBCA's defensive basketball drills / Women's Basketball Coaches Association.
    p. cm.
    ISBN 0-7360-3804-3
    1. Basketball for women--Defense. 2. Basketball for women--Coaching. I. Title:
Defensive basketball drills. II. Women's Basketball Coaches Association.
GV888.W33 2001
796.323'2--dc21

                                                                                    2001016566

ISBN: 0-7360-3804-3

Managing Editor: Melinda Graham; **Assistant Editor:** Scott Hawkins; **Consultants:** Kelly Hill, Todd Jensen; **Copyeditor:** Denelle Eknes; **Proofreader:** Susan C. Hagan; **Graphic Designer:** Nancy Rasmus; **Graphic Artist:** Francine Hamerski; **Photo Editor:** Clark Brooks; **Cover Designer:** Jack W. Davis; **Photographer (cover):** Tom Roberts; **Photographer (interior):** pp. xii, 90, and 120 Human Kinetics/Tom Roberts; p. 30 Human Kinetics/Clark Brooks; p. 60 Steve Woltman/SportsChrome USA; p. 142 ©iphotonews.com; and p. 168 Jay Crihfield/Spurlock Photography/Joe Robbins Photography; **Illustrator:** Tom Roberts; **Printer:** United Graphics

Human Kinetics books are available at special discounts for bulk purchase. Special editions or book excerpts can also be created to specification. For details, contact the Special Sales Manager at Human Kinetics.

Printed in the United States of America   10 9 8 7 6 5 4 3 2 1

Human Kinetics
Web site: www.humankinetics.com

United States: Human Kinetics, P.O. Box 5076, Champaign, IL 61825-5076
800-747-4457
e-mail: humank@hkusa.com

Canada: Human Kinetics, 475 Devonshire Road Unit 100, Windsor, ON N8Y 2L5
800-465-7301 (in Canada only)
e-mail: hkcan@mnsi.net

Europe: Human Kinetics, Units C2/C3 Wira Business Park, West Park Ring Road,
Leeds LS16 6EB, United Kingdom
+44 (0) 113 278 1708
e-mail: hk@hkeurope.com

Australia: Human Kinetics, 57A Price Avenue, Lower Mitcham, South Australia 5062
(08) 8277 1555
e-mail: liahka@senet.com.au

New Zealand: Human Kinetics, P.O. Box 105-231, Auckland Central
09-523 3462
e-mail: hkp@ihug.co.nz

CONTENTS

DRILL FINDER

FOREWORD

There is no substitute for hard work and no shortcuts to success, but with the right focus, proper preparation, and sufficient determination you can reach your goals. Defense must be a priority, and the *WBCA's Defensive Basketball Drills* book is one tool to help you accomplish what you're seeking.

Whether you're focusing on footwork or rebounding, you'll find something in this book to help you. The contributions of 28 top coaches will help boost skill development to a higher level. Make the most of the 92 proven drills in this book and you'll be on your way to a winning season.

Most successful coaches probably agree with the time-tested statement that offense sells tickets, but defense wins games. Playing defense well is an ever-changing chess match to stop new and innovative sets through smart play, intense effort, and execution of essential defensive skills.

The Women's Basketball Coaches Association constantly searches for ways to serve its entire membership. This defensive manual should be a major help to coaches and players at all levels of competition. The WBCA and I hope you'll find this book to be an asset to your basketball success.

Marsha Sharp

Marsha Sharp
Vice-president, WBCA

INTRODUCTION

"Offense sells tickets, but defense wins games." Consistently successful basketball players and teams know this coaching cliché to be true. So when it comes to developing their skills and tactics, players work on the defense in every practice. They don't ask why or when, they ask how.

Now, the "how" is found in this book. *WBCA's Defensive Basketball Drills* explains and illustrates 92 of the best drills that are in some way related to the goal of stopping an offensive opponent.

The footwork drills in chapter 1 are the first step to sound positioning and movement fundamentals. A good grasp of where to be and how to get there is essential to guarding an opposing player and reacting to help a teammate.

In chapter 2, the screening drills will help you disrupt the opposition's attempts to run two-player sets and offensive patterns. Players must know whether to go over the top, fight through, or switch when screens are set, and these drills will sharpen defenders' abilities to anticipate and stymie all types of offensive picks.

Nothing is more discouraging than to play 30 seconds of solid defense in which you force the opposition to take a poor shot, then fail to get the rebound. Defensive rebounding is essential as both the final piece of the defensive package and the start of an offensive break. Frequent and intense work on the rebounding drills in chapter 3 will improve performance on the boards.

Chapters 4 and 5 provide a wealth of drills to work on and polish players' defensive perimeter and post skills. You'll also find drills to prepare to stop the popular offensive inside-outside tactics used in today's game.

The transition game seems to become more important every season, as offenses pick up the pace and try to beat any defensive pressure. Chapter 6 includes may drills and teaching points to make sure players get back to stop the ball, and also turn the tables on the offense by eliminating their preferred options and quick-scoring opportunities.

The last chapter presents 15 drills to put the "team" stamp on your defensive approach. Footwork, rebounding, perimeter and post pressure, screen management, and transition defense are combined in integrated drills to coordinate the individual players on defensive units, and help become a singular force instead of five separate pieces.

This book along with its companion *WBCA's Offensive Basketball Drills* offer you a special collection of practice activities and coaching points to develop and hone individual and team performance on both ends of the court. Being sound fundamentally doesn't increase you're chances of making the TV highlights, but does make it much more likely that you'll be cutting down the nets at the end of the season.

KEY TO DIAGRAMS

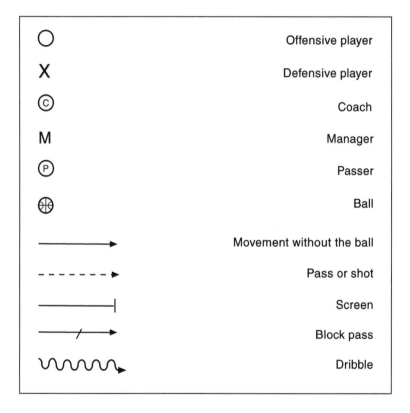

○	Offensive player
X	Defensive player
Ⓒ	Coach
M	Manager
Ⓟ	Passer
⊕	Ball
→	Movement without the ball
- - - ▸	Pass or shot
——⊢	Screen
⟋→	Block pass
∿∿∿▸	Dribble

FOOTWORK DRILLS

If you believe the adage, "offense sells tickets, but defense wins games," then you'll probably agree that sound footwork is the basis for any successful defense. Footwork can be taught, learned, and improved more than any other skill, yet it is often overlooked for other parts of the game.

Successful players in today's game have sound footwork and depend on it heavily to get them into proper position for on-ball or off-ball coverage responsibilities. They may also have outstanding quickness, great leaping ability, or incredible anticipation, but the best defenders all have outstanding footwork.

The drills presented in this section and throughout the book are from the top defensive coaches in the country. Follow their breakdowns and learn how to make footwork fun, challenging, and rewarding. These coaches expect to develop excellent players with the defensive abilities to win games. Build your program similarly, and perhaps you'll enjoy the rewards and longevity that go with the knowledge that, "offense sells tickets, but defense wins games!"

X Step

Coach Jane Albright
School University of Wisconsin

Purpose
To teach proper footwork for defending low post when fronting or going over the top.

Organization
Four players (two passers on the perimeter, an offensive and defensive low-post player), one ball.

Procedure
1. Start with the offensive and defensive players in low post on the left side and two passers on the perimeter at the wing and baseline.
2. Start the ball at the wing. The defender is in 3/4 denial on the high side of the low post.
3. On a pass to the baseline, the defender steps over the offense with her right foot to the front, then the post. She reverse pivots on her right foot and pulls her left foot through to deny on the baseline side.
4. On a pass from the baseline back to the wing, her left foot steps through to the front post; then she pulls her right foot through and back to the original 3/4 denial position.

Coaching Points
- Have the defender keep the space between herself and the offensive player to prevent her from posting the defender up or pinning on a reverse pass.
- Move on the pass—using two quick steps is the most efficient.

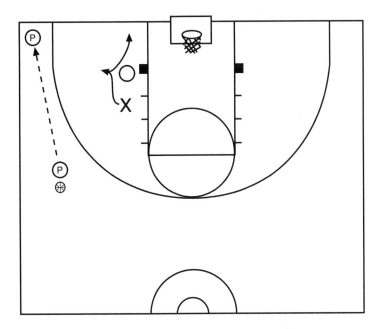

Chase

Coach Jane Albright
School University of Wisconsin

Purpose
To develop defensive quickness, balance, and the ability to change directions quickly.

Organization
Four players, four cones.

Procedure
1. Start players at cones A, B, C, and D.
2. Players will sprint from cone A to B.
3. Players will slide from cone B to C.
4. Players will backpedal from cone C to D.
5. Players will slide from cone D to A.
6. Players try to catch the person in front of them; if they are successful the player who was caught drops out. Play until one player is left or for a set time.

Coaching Points
- Stay low on slides, keeping the feet apart.
- Keep the weight forward on the backpedal to avoid falling back.
- Stay on the outside of the cones.

Variations
- Reverse directions. Sprint from cone D to C.
- Slide from cone C to B.
- Backpedal from cone B to A.
- Slide from cone A to D.

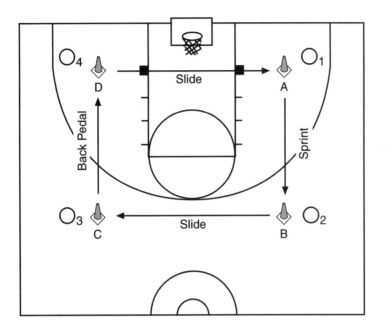

Lane Closeouts

Coach Jane Albright
School University of Wisconsin

Purpose

To work on different aspects of defense, such as slides, closeouts, backpedals, and sprints. To close out under control, without lunging.

Organization

Two to three players at each basket, starting under the basket on the baseline.

Procedure

1. One player at a time starts on the baseline or on the right side facing the foul line. The player closes out against an imaginary offensive player on the right side, faces with her foot, and backpedals to the baseline, with her hands above her head.

2. She closes out to the foul line again. This time she pivots and sprints to the basket, then jumps up to touch the backboard or net.

3. She closes out a third time to the foul line. She touches it with her foot, drop steps, and slides to the baseline.

4. The next player starts.

5. Repeat these three steps three times.

Coaching Points

- On the closeout, sprint out and shuffle to the foul line on the last step or two, with hands high.
- Stay balanced on the backpedal and low on the slides.
- Maintain the proper closeout position while moving, with the body always in control.

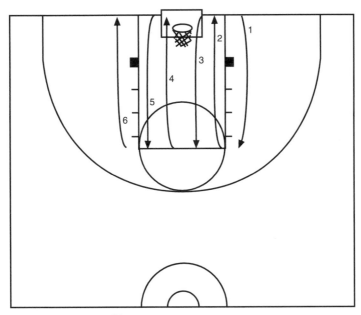

1 Close out
2 Backpedal
3 Close out
4 Sprint and touch backboard/net
5 Close out
6 Drop step-slide

Closeout Drill

Coach Cindy Anderson
School Loyola College

Purpose

To improve defenders' help-side defense by recovering quickly. To close out the shooter and react to dribble penetration.

Organization

Half of the team at each end in line under the basket, one ball at each end.

Procedure

1. The first two players in line step out. The offensive player is at the wing outside the three-point line.
2. The defensive player is in help position, seeing both the ball and player.
3. The coach has the ball at the three-point line on the opposite wing.
4. The coach skip passes to the offensive player who looks to shoot or drive.
5. The defensive player closes out on offense (runs out) with a high hand close enough to prevent a shot.
6. The defensive player is forcing the ball to the corner.

Coaching Points

- Stay low on the closeout; don't hop or jump stop into the offense.
- Hold the high hand straight up and keep the butt down.
- Direct the offensive players to drive to the baseline, but not open too much.

Variations

- Use posts in this drill to work on mobility and zone slides.
- Box out and rebound to work on playing hard to the end.

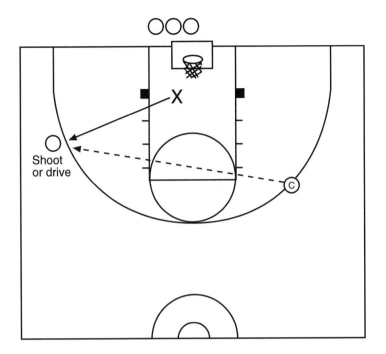

Shoot or drive

Move Your Feet!

Coach Cindy Anderson
School Loyola College

Purpose
To help players recover when getting beat off the dribble.

Organization
Four players (two on offense, two on defense), one ball with a coach on the wing.

Procedure
1. The coach passes the ball to O_1 (X_1 denies this but lets offense catch the ball for the sake of the drill).
2. O_1 beats X_1 off the dribble going to her left.
3. X_1 drop steps off her player and slides over to stop ball penetration of O_1.
4. Once the ball is stopped, X_1 can recover to her player, and X_2 goes back to denying her player O_2 the ball.
5. Repeat from several angles to the basket (i.e., wing to post, post to post, guard to post).

Coaching Points
- Stay low, keep hands active, communicate on screens, and maintain good body balance.
- The defender who lost the ball should communicate that she has recovered so her teammate can go back to her player.
- Communicate!

Variation
- Advance to three on three; help and recover using the same principles.

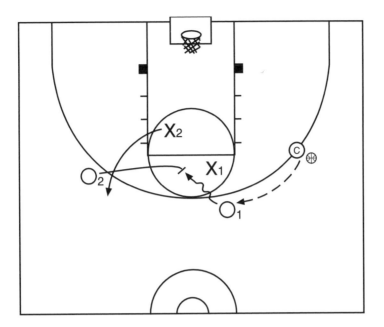

Shell Drill With Towels

Coach Ceal Barry
School University of Colorado

Purpose
To help defensive players understand their positioning in relation to the ball and their offensive players as offense is setting screens. Emphasize moving feet and not just reaching with hands.

Organization
Four offensive and four defensive players, one ball. After the series, change offense to defense, with defense out and four new players on offense. Defensive players each have a towel around their necks and are holding the ends of the towels.

Procedure
1. Offensive players set up in a shell on the perimeter, two guards and two forwards.
2. Player O_1 passes to player O_2 (see diagram 1).
3. Player O_1, making the pass, screens down for player O_3 (see diagram 2).
4. X_1 creates space for X_3 to get through the screen.

Coaching Points
- Teach proper spacing—(1) on ball, (2) the defender one pass away is in the passing lane, and (3) the defender two passes away is in help-side defense.
- The defender of the player setting the screen must call the screen and create space for her teammate to get through.
- Footwork is critical because hands are eliminated from this drill.

Variations
- Add back screens, cross screens, give and go cut.
- Add a post player.

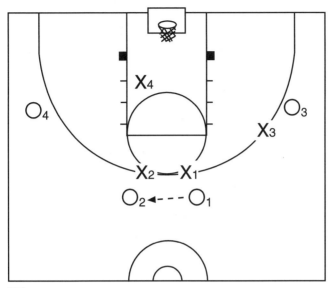

1

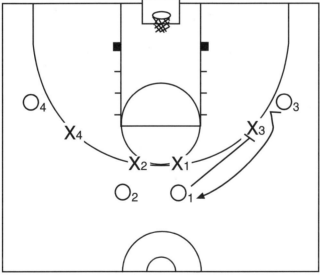

2

Three on Three—
Balance and Contain

Coach Carol Hammerle
School Northern Illinois University

Purpose
To work on both defensive and offensive skills. Defensively, this drill encourages players to focus on their footwork and teaches them containment. Offensively, it is a great drill to practice controlling the ball and making strong passes off the dribble.

Organization
Six players (three offensive and three defensive), one ball, three lanes.

Procedure
1. Three offensive and three defensive players begin on the baseline and must move the ball full court, within their respective lanes, to the opposite baseline.
2. Allow the offensive players only one dribble before they must pass. The ball should start in the middle and move from side to side. Offensive players remain in their lane.
3. Defensively, players are working for on-the-ball defense, one pass away, and help-side defense footwork and communication.
4. The drill is complete when the offense reaches the opposite baseline. If there is a steal or turnover, reward the defense by making them offense.
5. Rotate offense to defense.

Coaching Points
- Defensively, have players work on staying balanced and not reaching for the ball. Concentrate on vision, containment, and communication.
- Because you are allowing the offensive player only one dribble, this drill is great for teaching players to handle the ball under extreme pressure.
- Offensive players must pass to the hand away from the defense.

Variations
- Allow two dribbles for offensive players when starting with inexperienced players.
- Make no restrictions on the number of dribbles for offensive players.

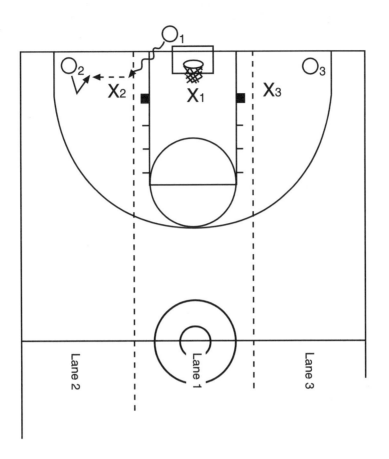

Perimeter Closeout

Coach Kris Huffman
School Depaw University

Purpose

To help defensive players improve closeout technique and positioning. The defender is attempting to take away the outside shot, the look inside, and the middle penetration with the pressure she applies.

Organization

Twelve players, five balls, a coach passing to the top of the key. Three offensive players line up on each side of the three-point line; three defenders start in the lane. The next three defenders are ready to enter the lane when vacated.

Procedure

1. The coach at the top of the key slaps the ball to start the drill. The three defenders in the lane drop into a stance and stutter step.
2. The coach passes to either side. The three defenders close out to the offensive players.
3. The top offensive player passes back to the coach. The three defenders jump to the ball, then become the offensive players. The offensive players join the defensive line on the baseline.
4. The next three defenders are in the lane stuttering when the coach has the ball on top of the key. The coach passes to the other side and the drill continues.

Coaching Points

- The defenders must close out in a stance with the inside foot and hand up.
- The offensive players must be active with the ball—triple threat; jab while the defender pressures the ball.

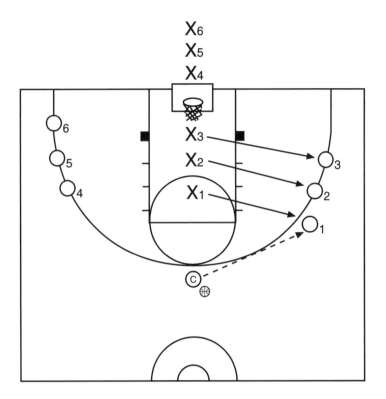

9 Block Drill

Coach Yvonne Kauffman
School Elizabethtown College

Purpose
To develop conditioning and defensive stance.

Organization
Players in even groups with four blocks of wood (hand size) per group.

Procedure
1. Place the wooden blocks on the key, one in the middle of the foul line, one on each of the low blocks.
2. A player holds the fourth wooden block.
3. The coach times 30 seconds or a predetermined time.
4. The player side slides from one block to the opposite block, drops the block in hand, and picks up the block on the floor.
5. The player sprints to the foul line, drops the block, and picks up a new block on the floor.
6. The player slides back to the low block where she began, drops her block, and picks up the other block.
7. Continue this for 30 seconds.

Coaching Points
- Keep the body low.
- Accelerate from block to block.

Variations
- Have contests.

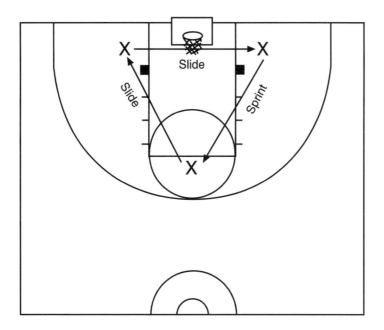

Super Denial

Coach Muffet McGraw
School University of Notre Dame

Purpose

To improve guards' reaction time from denying a pass to the wing to defending the backdoor cut.

Organization

One offensive player on the wing, one offensive player on the block, one defensive player denying on the wing, one coach with a rack of balls at the top of the key.

Procedure

1. The coach makes a pass to the wing. The defender knocks the pass away and immediately slides or shuffles to the block to defend the pass from the coach to the block (see diagram 1).

2. After knocking the pass away to the block, the defender slides or shuffles back to knock away the pass to the wing (see diagram 2).

3. Repeat eight times.

Coaching Points

- Emphasize quickly turning the head, pushing off hard with the outside leg, and keeping the hand out in the passing lane.
- The coach must have a rack of balls to fire the passes quickly.

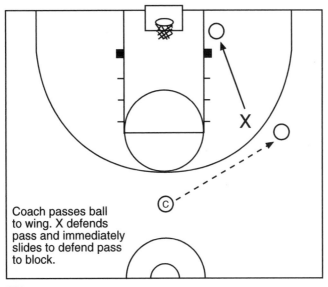

Coach passes ball
to wing. X defends
pass and immediately
slides to defend pass
to block.

1

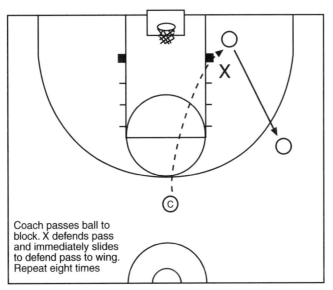

Coach passes ball to
block. X defends pass
and immediately slides
to defend pass to wing.
Repeat eight times

2

Defensive Series

Coach Jody Rajcula
School Western Connecticut State University

Purpose
To teach defending the wing pop out, backdoor cut, weak-side baseline, strong-side elbow, and high to low post cuts.

Organization
Three or four players per basket.

Procedure
1. Player O_2 has the ball at the high wing. Player X_1 is guarding player O_1 at her strong-side back.
2. Player O_1 pops out to catch a pass, and player X_1 denies her (if open, O_1 gets the pass and squares up, then passes back) (see diagram 1).
3. Player O_1 then cuts through the backdoor to the opposite low baseline.
4. Player X_1 must defend the backdoor by either opening up or turning her head (see diagram 2).
5. Player O_1 then cuts from weak-side baseline to strong-side elbow (see diagram 3).
6. Player X_1 must defend (step up to deny at the high post).
7. Player O_2 dribbles out to the wing. Player O_1 cuts from high to low post. Player X_1 must defend as shown in diagram 4 (open up and slide down to deny on the high side at the block).
8. Player O_2 then dribbles up and the drill repeats.

Coaching Points
- Teach all the defensive positions as walk-throughs first.
- Go through them three or four times. If an offensive player catches the ball, she passes it back to player O_2, and the drill continues.

Variations
- The defensive player defends until she deflects the ball six times.
- You can also put defense on passer O_2.
- If you don't have enough baskets, divide the team by the number of baskets. Use four players (two passers). If you have more players, rotate them.
- Start the drill on the opposite side of the floor so players learn to defend the other side of the floor.

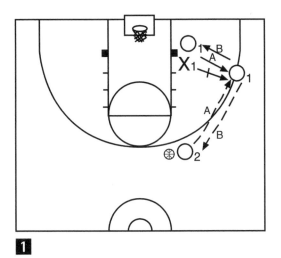

1

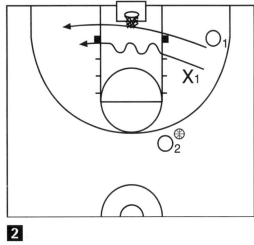

2

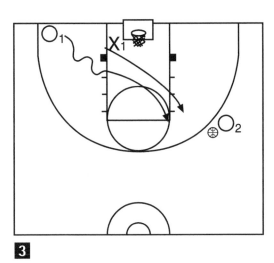

3

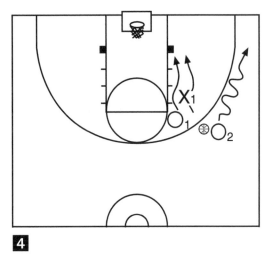

4

HOB (Head on Ball)

Coach Jody Rajcula
School Western Connecticut State University

Purpose
To put full-court pressure on the ball and force the offense to change directions as much as possible.

Organization
Two groups of perimeter players on the baseline (baseline divided in half). The drill only goes to half court.

Procedure
1. X_1 is defense and faces O_1 with the ball on the baseline.
2. O_1 has only half the court and tries to dribble to the midcourt line.
3. X_1 concentrates on keeping her head on the ball and tries to turn O_1 as many times as possible before midcourt.
4. If the ball is loose, both players must hustle after it.
5. Offense and defense switch as they come back to the end of the line on baseline.

Coaching Points
- Must stress low defensive position. X_1 positions her head on the ball.
- Her inside hand tries to make steals on all crossovers and spins—no hand checking.
- Her feet must slide, not cross. Keep the hands outside the knees, and don't lunge!

Variations
- See how many turns the defense can force before half court.
- Add two defensive players to work on trapping.

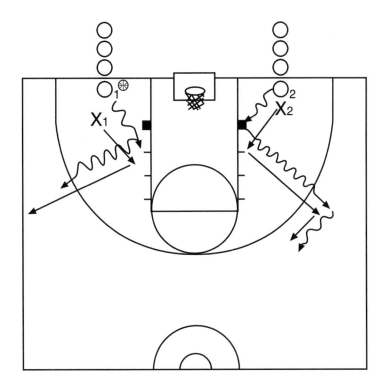

One-on-One Full Court

Coach Tim Shea
School Salem State College

Purpose
To teach players to never allow the dribbler to get by them.

Organization
Two players and one ball on each side of the court.

Procedure
1. One player on offense is defended by a second player.
2. The defender forces the dribbler to use her weak hand at all times.
3. The dribbler *must* try to get by her defender, and if she does, she speed dribbles to the end of the court.
4. Boundary lines are the sideline and the free throw lane line extended. The middle of the court is where the coaches stand.
5. Players switch (offense to defense) at the far end of the court for the return trip.
6. Each player goes three times, and do this drill every other practice.

Coaching Points
- Use these defensive principles on the perimeter only, not in scoring areas.
- A defender is most likely to be beat on a dribbler's initial move. The defender should back off until the dribbler puts the ball on the floor, then tighten up the distance between the defender and the ball.
- Once a defender learns how far off the ball she should be, she must maintain that distance. If the dribbler gets too close, the defender does not have the correct spacing.
- When a dribbler gets going with her weak hand, don't shut her down. This will force her to use her strong hand! Instead, stay in a defensive position and allow the dribbler to keep using her weak hand.
- Players should not go against the same opponent every time.
- This drill serves as an excellent dribbling drill too.

Variation
- Try to force the dribbler to change directions as many times as possible, but do not let the dribbler beat the defense.

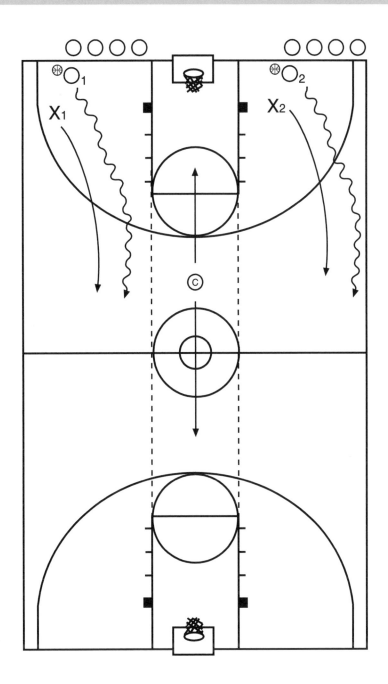

Turn and Channel

Coach Pat Summitt
School University of Tennessee

Purpose

To teach players how to pick up the ball full court, force the dribbler to turn at least once before the ball gets to half court, then channel the offensive player down the sideline.

Organization

As many players as you like. Each pair of players has a ball and two lines (one on each side of the floor on either baseline).

Procedure

1. Pair up the players with similar physical abilities.
2. The offensive players begin to dribble up the floor.
3. The defensive player gets in the offensive player's way and makes her change direction.
4. The defensive player tries to force two or three turns.
5. Once the ball is across the half-court line, the defender channels the offensive player down the sideline.
6. The offensive player tries to beat the defenders down the middle.

Coaching Points

- Have the dribbler start slow and make turns whether or not she is forced.
- Have the defender get in front of the dribbler with her head on the ball.
- Have the defender not allow the dribbler to go across the floor in the half court.

Variation

- Once the players know how the drill works, have the offensive player go full speed to see if the defender can influence where the ball goes.

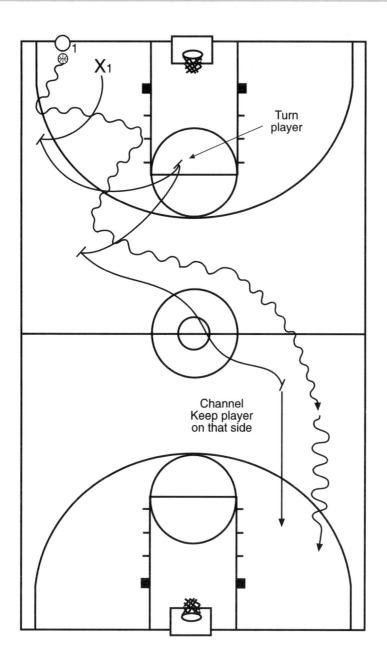

SCREENING DRILLS

Screen and roll, give and go, dive and cut—without these tactics how would an offense begin to attack a strong defensive team? Most scouting reports can give a coach the patterns and tendencies of the opponent, but nothing can replace the day-to-day drilling and preparation players must do so they can read and react properly to screening situations.

Connecticut, Duke, Louisiana Tech, and other top programs owe much of their defensive success to reading and reacting properly in game screening situations. Motion offenses give players a lot of freedom that can challenge an unprepared defensive team. However, communication, anticipation, team concept, and unselfish play allow players to apply pressure or provide help at just the right time.

In this chapter, you'll learn how to break down the opponents' screens and take them out of their offensive patterns. Daily drilling on your screening principles will allow players to feel comfortable in any situation, knowing they can depend on one another to communicate, anticipate, and play unselfishly.

UCLA Cut

Coach Cindy Anderson
School Loyola College

Purpose
To defend front cuts and work on jumping to the ball.

Organization
One-half of the team at each end, one ball, one line at the top of the key.

Procedure
1. The ball is at the top of the key with O_1. X_1 is defending, forcing her player to the corner.
2. O_1 passes to the coach on the wing and tries to front cut.
3. X_1 jumps to the ball and forces O_1 to cut behind her.
4. X_1 opens up to the ball, following O_1 down the lane.
5. The coach tries to pass to O_1.
6. X_1 needs a deflection or a steal to get off the court.

Coaching Points
- The defense needs to stay low.
- The defense needs to follow and feel offense through, seeing the ball at the same time.

Variations
- O_1 can post up on the block; X_1 needs to front.
- Move offensive cutting line to the wing (where the coach was) and the coach to the corner. Have the pass go to the coach. The offense tries to front out; the defender jumps to the ball and forces offense to cut behind.

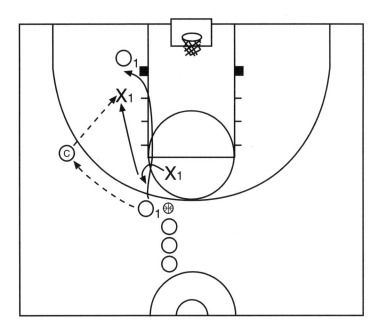

Step Back—Get Through

Coach Cindy Anderson
School Loyola College

Purpose
To get through screens occurring off the ball.

Organization
Three offensive players, three defenders, using both ends of the court. The three offensive players start with the ball at the top and two wings.

Procedure
1. O_2 passes to O_1 and screens for O_3.
2. X_2 steps back and lets X_3 (who is getting screened) through.
3. Once X_3 gets through, she must be on the line or up the line to prevent the curl cut to the basket by O_3.
4. X_1 maintains good guarding position on the O_1 passer.

Coaching Points
- Communicate on impending screens.
- Help teammates through the screen by stepping back and pulling their shirts to help them get through.
- Recover in the passing lane, ready to prevent the cutter from receiving the ball.

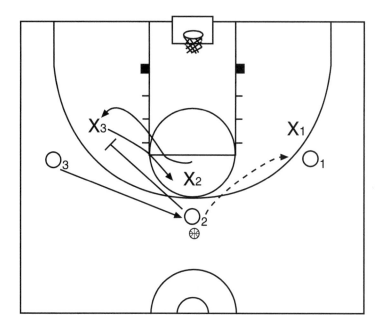

Two-on-Two Screen Defense

Coach Ceal Barry
School University of Colorado

Purpose
To help defenders understand getting through screens.

Organization
Two offensive players, two defensive players, one coach with the ball. Rotate offense to defense; defense goes out and new offensive players come in.

Procedure
1. The coach has the ball on the wing.
2. The ball side post, O_5, sets a cross screen on X_4 for the opposite post, O_4 (see diagram 1).
3. X_5 calls the screen, then positions herself in the path of the player cutting to the ball (she bumps the cutter).
4. X_4 works around the other side of the screen and gets into proper off-ball defensive position on her player who was slowed down by her teammate (see diagram 2).

Coaching Points
- Start in the proper position; see your player and the ball.
- Be vocal—call screens.
- The defender of the player setting the screen must beat the cutter to a spot on the floor and make her go around.
- The defender of the cutter must quickly get into position and release her teammate back to her player.

Variations
- Add down screens.
- Add back screens.
- Add a second passer.

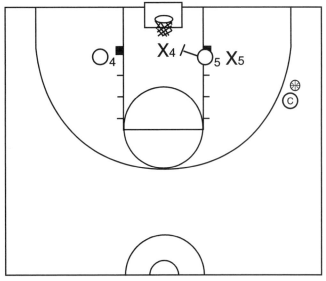

1

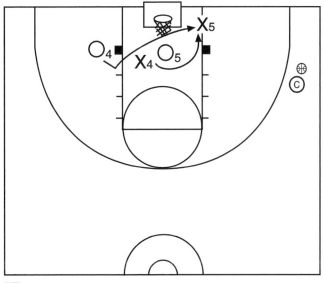

2

Change Drill

Coach Ceal Barry
School University of Colorado

Purpose
To create gamelike situations of defending screens while rewarding the defense. To react quickly in the defensive position and to slow or stop the ball.

Organization
Five offensive players in a shell, five defensive players, one ball, shot clock, scorekeeper.

Procedure
1. Offensive players set up in a shell (either four perimeters and one post or three perimeters and two posts).
2. Offense can down screen and cross screen but always fill the original shell (see diagram 1).
3. The defenders call the screens and create space for teammates to get through the screens (see diagram 2).
4. Defense scores 2 points for a steal or a charge, 1 point for deflection.
5. After 20 seconds on the shot clock, the coach yells, "Change." Offense sets the ball down; the defender picks it up and goes in transition to the opposite end (see diagram 3).
6. Each defender must now guard a player other than the one who was guarding her. Run a 30-second clock for this possession, again scoring points for defense.
7. Start the drill again in a half-court shell for 20 seconds.

Coaching Points
- Teach proper positioning on defense.
- Be vocal—call screens.
- Create the space for teammates to get through the screen.
- Teach defensive transition—stopping the ball in transition.

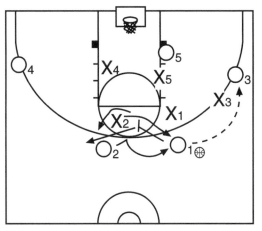

1

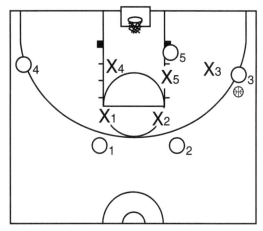

2

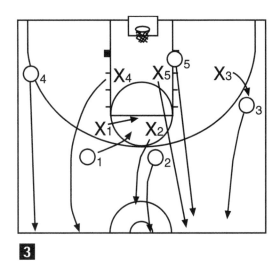

3

Coach Nikki Caldwell
School University of Virginia

Purpose
To help players recognize and defend screens on the ball with rotation from the help side.

Organization
Six players, three offense and three defense on the perimeter, one ball.

Procedure
1. Players are three on three on the perimeter.
2. O_1 passes to either O_2 or O_3. O_1 then goes to set a screen on the ball (see diagram 1).
3. Weak-side defense must jump to the help side.
4. The player on the wing with the ball uses the screen and attacks the middle.
5. The defensive player on the ball and the defensive player guarding the person setting the screen will then trap the wing (see diagram 2).
6. The weak-side defender on the help side will read the situation and try to steal the pass made to the person who has rolled off the screen.
7. Don't give up a layup. The weak-side defender will have to play both her player and the person who has set the screen.
8. If the pass is made out of the trap, the defensive player who was initially screened will rotate out of the trap and find the open player.

Coaching Points
- Weak-side defender, get off to the help side. Look to steal the ball, but don't give up a layup.
- Defense, communicate on all screens.
- Set a good trap, but don't allow the offense to split the trap.

Variation
- Three on three could consist of a player up top, a player on the wing, and a player on the block.

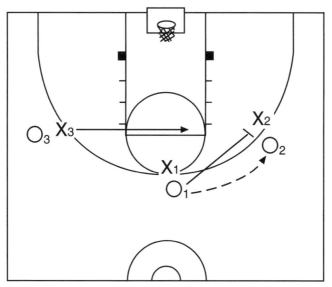

1

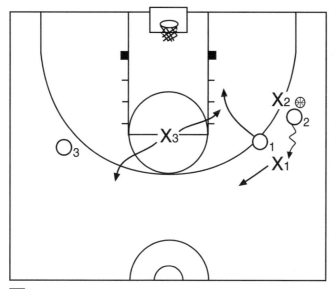

2

20

Defending Down Screens From the Top

Coach Carol Hammerle
School Northern Illinois University

Purpose

To teach defending down screens with the ball below the free throw line extended. This drill provides repetition in defending the pass and screen away. The objective in defending this screen is to prevent the shot, then stop and slow the ball reversal by getting into the passing lane.

Organization

Four players (two offensive and two defensive), one ball, one coach.

Procedure

1. O_1 passes to the coach and sets the screen in the lane on X_2.
2. X_1 drops quickly, opens to the ball, and protects the basket.
3. X_2 fights over the screen to contest the reversal pass.
4. If the ball is entered, the offensive players rescreen.
5. Once the ball is entered to an offensive player, the drill is live with a ball screen at the top.

Coaching Points

- X_1 must jump to the line after the ball is passed to the coach to prevent a front cut (give and go).
- X_1 must leave room for teammate X_2 to get over the screen. The player defending the screener always defends the basket.

Variation

- The defender being screened should focus on moving the lead (top) leg first. Unless the offensive player flares, the defender should go over the ball side (top) of the screen to maintain the ball-me-player relationship on defense.

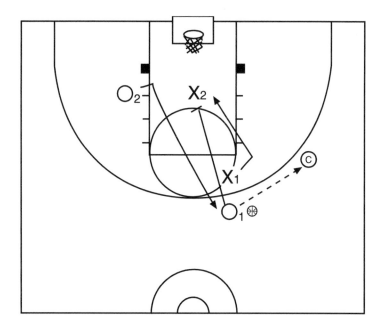

21 Defending Down Screens From the Side

Coach Carol Hammerle
School Northern Illinois University

Purpose
To practice the technique of defending a down screen. This drill allows repetition in a short time period.

Organization
Eight players (four offensive and four defensive), one ball, one coach.

Procedure
1. Players set up in a four-on-four situation with players on each wing and in both posts. The coach initiates the drill as the offensive players on the wing set down screens.
2. Defenders guarding screeners drop quickly, open to the ball, protect the basket, and close down to the line of the ball.
3. The defenders guarding the players receiving screens fight over the top of the screen to contest the entry pass.
4. If the ball isn't entered, the offensive players rescreen.
5. Once the ball is entered, the drill is live and ends with a four-on-four situation.

Coaching Points
- Although there is no rule for the defender to go over the top on a down screen (because the offensive player may flare to the baseline), the player being screened needs to move her lead leg over the screen to get through.
- The person defending the screener must leave a gap for her teammate to fight over the screen. The player defending the screener always defends the basket.
- Defenders should see the ball and their players at all times.

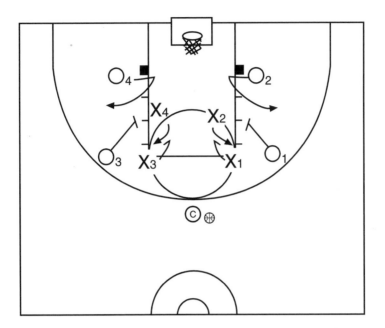

Middle One Out

Coach Carol Hammerle
School Northern Illinois University

Purpose

To practice defending down screens from either side, depending on offensive players' use of the screen.

Organization

Six players (three offensive and three defensive), one ball, one coach.

Procedure

1. Players set up in a three-on-three situation with offense and defense on each wing, and in the middle of the lane.
2. Offensive wing players (O_1 and O_2) screen down for player O_3 in the middle.
3. Defensive players X_1, X_2, and X_3 must handle the screening situation according to defensive rules.
4. If an offensive player doesn't receive an entry pass, she goes back down to receive a screen.
5. The middle player goes out to either side.
6. The coach can enter a pass at any time and the drill becomes live.

Coaching Points

- The ball is above the free throw line, so the defenders guarding each screener should be on and up the line to allow room for the person defending the middle player. Stay high and go over the top of the screen rather than chasing.
- If the offensive player flares, the defender can decide if she should go over the top or below the screen.

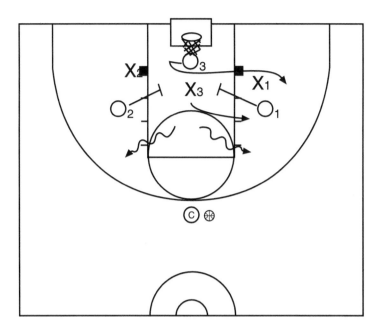

Back Screens

Coach Andy Landers
School University of Georgia

Purpose
To teach players to set, use, and defend back screens.

Organization
Two offensive and two defensive players, one on the wing and one on the block, one coach with the ball.

Procedure
1. O_1 drives her player away from the impending screen from O_2, setting her player up.
2. O_2 comes up to screen for O_1 (giving one step to defender if this is a blind screen [rule]).
3. O_2 screens X_1 from the rear. O_1 makes a quick, hard cut to the basket.
4. O_2 rolls back toward the ball after screening.
5. X_1 and X_2 communicate and work together to defend the screen.

Coaching Points
- Give the defender a step to avoid contact on all blind or rear screens.
- Roll back to the ball after screening defense.

Variation
- Players can combine double screens and back screens into one drill, teaching communication and taking it into two-on-two play.

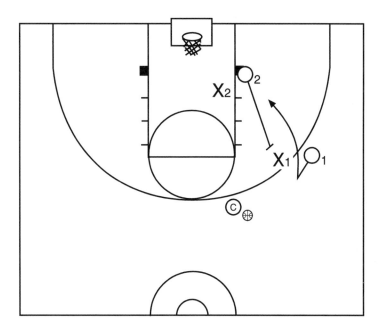

Down Screens

Coach Andy Landers
School University of Georgia

Purpose
To teach players how to set down screens and how to defend these screens.

Organization
Two lines (one out of bounds near the block and the other on the wing), one coach with the ball at the top. It is two on two, with offense and defense on wing and underneath.

Procedure
1. O_1 will start on wing and will come down to set the screen for O_2 on the block.
2. O_2 will get her defender (X_2) up by driving her under the basket, then waiting for the screen to be set before cutting hard off the screen.
3. O_1 rolls back toward the coach with the ball.
4. The defenders communicate and work together to get through screens.
5. Offense goes to defense; defense goes out to the end of different offensive lines.

Coaching Points
- Set the defensive player up by driving her under the basket as the screen is being set.
- The screener should put her belly button on the hip of the defender.
- The screener always rolls back to the ball.

Variation
- Play two on two live after a certain number of down screens.

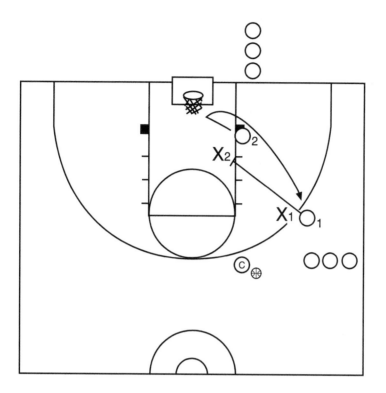

Coach Andy Landers
School University of Georgia

Purpose

To teach players how to set legal screens for a ball handler, how to roll to get open, and how to defend the screens.

Organization

Three offensive players, three defensive players, one ball, lines behind each of the three offensive players. Start one offensive player at the top of the key and one on each wing.

Procedure

1. O_1 starts with ball at the top and passes to O_2 (see diagram 1).
2. O_1 follows the pass and screens on the ball for O_2.
3. O_2 dribbles over the screen. O_1 rolls hard (defense may fight over the top or step through—your philosophy dictates).
4. O_2 gets to the top and passes to O_3 (see diagram 2).
5. O_2 follows the pass and screens on the ball for O_3. O_2 rolls.
6. Continue for four to five repetitions, and rotate offense to defense, defense to the back of a different line.

Coaching Points

- Set a solid, strong screen with the belly button on the hip.
- The defense must communicate to deal with screens effectively.
- Work with defense on getting over screens, switching, or sliding under.
- Emphasize the roll, good contact, and the target hand.

Variations

- Hit the roll with a pass if open—defense defends.
- Play three on three live after four screens.

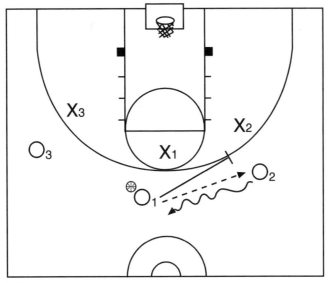

1

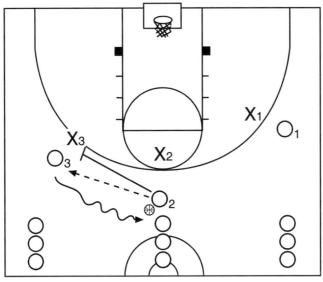

2

Defending Ball Screens

Coach Kay Yow
School North Carolina State University

Purpose
To force the ball handler out wide and allow the defender time to fight over the top of the screen.

Organization
Four players, one ball, and two lines. Guards are in a line at the wing, and posts are in a line under the basket near the block. The first person in line is defense and the second person in line is offense. Players rotate from offense to defense to the end of their line.

Procedure
1. X_1 and X_2 take proper player-to-player positions, based on the position of the ball and their defensive assignments.
2. O_2 sets a screen on the ball for O_1. O_1 tries to use the screen and get to the basket.
3. X_2 gets to the high side of the screen, forcing the ball handler to take an arched path to the basket.
4. X_1 turns and sprints through the screen and beats the ball handler to the spot, not allowing her to turn the corner and get to the basket.
5. X_2 has helped and must recover quickly as X_1 recovers back to the ball.

Note. If the screen is guard-guard or post-post, switch on the screen.

Coaching Points
- Good timing as well as good communication between players is essential.
- Post player hedging must be at a 90-degree angle to the direction the ball handler is heading. If the body position is too open, the dribbler will have a direct path to the basket.
- The defender on the ball must turn and sprint through the screen to the spot the ball handler is heading (sliding is too slow).
- The post player must never lose touch with her defensive assignment. She should keep one hand on the offensive player's hip and the other out, up, and wide.

Variations
- Do the drill from various spots on the floor.
- Have the guard on the ball go behind the screen as the post player bodies up.
- Trap the ball handler.

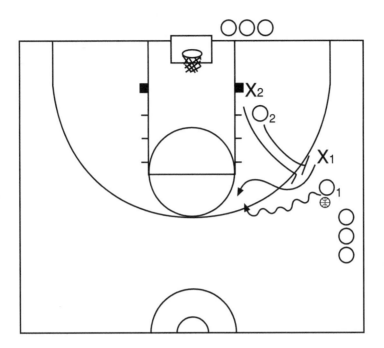

Defending Back Screens

Coach Kay Yow
School North Carolina State University

Purpose

To learn to defend a back screen using player-to-player principles and to recognize guard-guard, post-post, or guard-post screens.

Organization

Four players, one ball, and a line under the basket. Players are positioned on both the left elbow and left block, and a coach is positioned at the top of the key with a ball. Another coach is on the right wing. Players rotate up the line (defense on block to offense on block, offense on block to defense on elbow, defense on elbow to offense on elbow, offense on elbow to the end of the line).

Procedure

1. X_1 and X_2 take proper defensive positions in relation to the ball at the top of the key (see diagram 1).
2. The coach passes the ball to the coach on the right wing. X_1 and X_2 adjust their positions in relation to the ball and their defensive assignments.
3. As the coach on the wing receives the ball, O_2 sets a back screen for O_1 on the elbow (see diagram 2).
4. X_2 gets as close to O_2 as possible, leaving X_1 plenty of room to get through the screen. (As an option, depending on the offensive player, X_2 may drop off O_2 and put a hand in the passing lane until X_1 recovers to O_1. X_2 then recovers to O_2.)
5. X_1 rolls off the screen toward the ball with her hand up in the passing lane and meets O_1 on the block (see diagram 3).
6. X_2 will help X_1 if O_1 flares or kicks back off the screen.
7. If O_1 does flare or kick back, X_2 and X_1 need to help and recover quickly.

Note. If the screen is guard-guard or post-post, simply switch on the screen.

Coaching Points

- Players must communicate. Let teammates know the screen is coming. Recognize the type of screen (guard-guard, post-post, or guard-post).
- Using proper player-to-player defensive positions, try to avoid the screen altogether.
- If help is required, help and recover quickly.
- The defender being screened must always roll toward the ball with her hand up. This player needs to look big and cut down the passing angle.
- The player guarding the screener can help slow the offensive player using the screen by bumping the cutter.

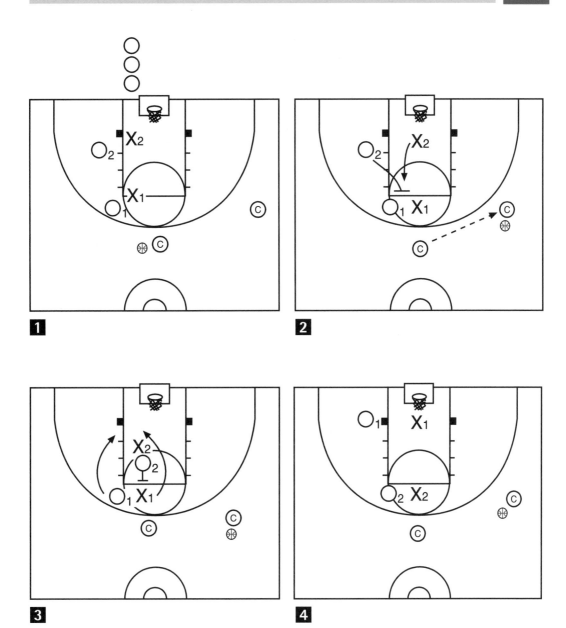

1

2

3

4

Continuous Cross Screens

Coach Kay Yow
School North Carolina State University

Purpose

To teach players to stay with their defensive assignments on screens that occur away from the ball by using solid player-to-player principles and positioning.

Organization

Three lines, one at the top of the key and one on each wing. The first player in each line is defense and the next player is offense. The offensive player at the top of the key starts the drill with a ball. Offense goes to defense, and defense rotates clockwise to the end of the next line.

Procedure

1. O_1 passes to O_2.
2. All the defensive players adjust their positions based on where the ball is.
3. After passing, O_1 goes away from the ball to set a screen on X_3.
4. X_1 sags toward the basket in her help spot as O_1 goes away from the ball. X_1 needs to be sure to leave X_3 enough room to slide through the screen.
5. X_3 takes a step backward toward the basket and slides through the screen to beat, or at least meet, O_3 at the top of the key.
6. X_3 is in a position to steel or knock the ball away.

Coaching Points

- Teach proper body position and angles.
- Stress the fundamentals of proper player-to-player defense. The defensive players must reposition themselves on every pass and jump to the ball.
- Teach players to see the screen coming so they can avoid the screen altogether.
- Stress the importance of communication between teammates.

Variation

- Have the wings V cut to get open and receive the ball. Once the screen is set, play live (three on three). Offense can score only off a cross screen.

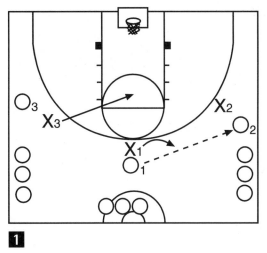

1

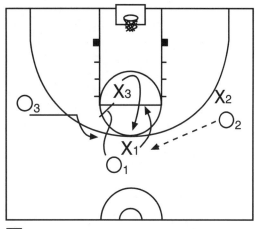

2

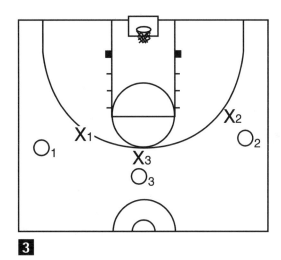

3

REBOUNDING DRILLS

Although it's obvious that big, strong, and tall players would form a good rebounding team, we've also seen our share of small, aggressive, and hard-nosed teams that have dominated the boards, allowing no second shots by their opponents. Defensive rebounding is both attitude and technique. A team of individuals who are dedicated to their rebounding assignment, and have the commitment and ability to make sure their player is not the one getting the ball, can frustrate a bigger, even taller team to no end.

Teaching the basic footwork of rebounding, and the inevitability of contact, gives coaches a lot to work with in building their defensive framework. Whether your team is big or small has nothing to do with the size of their hearts and their commitment to making sure their player does not get to a rebounded ball first.

Use the drills and techniques in this chapter to refine your defensive rebounding. These coaches know how to get the most out of their players and how to keep them focused on controlling the boards. Perhaps you'll pick up an idea that can help your players—big or small—earn the rebounds they deserve.

Game Time

Coach Gary Blair
School University of Arkansas

Purpose

To simulate a game situation of half-court rebounding, while encouraging offense to crash the boards. It is great for conditioning.

Organization

A coach with the ball, three lines underneath the goal, three offensive players on the court, three defensive players. A rebound ring creates realistic misses. You can use cones to mark where the players are to sprint.

Procedure

1. Offense assumes their position on the court relative to where the coach is with the ball.
2. Defense matches up with offense and assumes the defensive position that the coach desires (see diagram 1).
3. When the coach is satisfied with defense's positioning, the he takes the shot.
4. Defense calls, "shot," then they find, feel, and fly. Offense crashes the boards (see diagram 2).
5. If defense controls, they outlet and go three on zero to other end. Then they sprint around the court to the back of the lines.
6. If offense controls, they power it back in. Defense must sprint to the other end, then around the court to the back of the lines.

Coaching Points

- Demand that defense be in your desired positions before offense takes the shot.
- *Find* your player. *Feel* the contact. *Fly* to the ball.
- Teach players to read and react to the shot. Long shots equal long rebounds. Misses 60 percent of the time go to the weak side. Play the percentages.

Variations

- The coach moves to various spots to change the rebound angles.
- Make it competitive by keeping score.

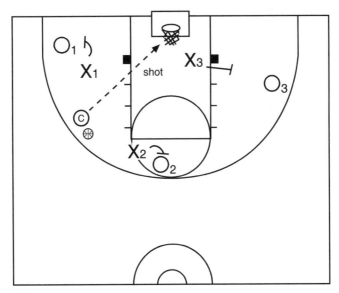

1

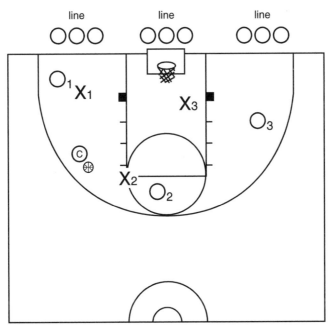

2

Coach Gary Blair
School University of Arkansas

Purpose

To teach good rebounding habits and sound technique; to reinforce proper timing and execution of a rebound.

Organization

One line on each side of the board, two balls in each line. You can vary this depending on the number of players and baskets.

Procedure

1. The first rebounder on each side tosses the ball off the glass and times the jump to catch the ball with both hands at the top of the jump.
2. The first rebounder on each side pivots and passes to the player at the outlet on her side of the floor.
3. The rebounder follows her pass to the outlet. The outlet player goes to the back of the opposite rebound line.
4. The next person in line becomes a rebounder for a continuous drill.
5. Repeat until everyone has grabbed 10 boards.

Coaching Points

- Demand proper technique *every time*, otherwise it is wasted time.
- "Z" the ball after grabbing the rebound with both hands to chinned position. This keeps the ball moving and discourages others from reaching in.

Variations

- Start with the rebounder facing away from the backboard, and have the next player in line toss the ball off the glass, to force her to turn and find the ball.
- Allow the outlet passer to take the dribble to the other end for a shot. This adds conditioning and shooting to maximize the drill.

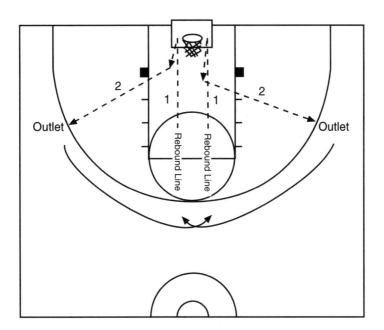

Weak–Side Crash

Coach Gary Blair
School University of Arkansas

Purpose

To teach players to crash weak-side boards from game-situation positions. To teach players to read and react to shots so they can create more rebounding opportunities.

Organization

Use a rebound ring to create realistic misses. Two lines form on the sideline where the coach is attempting a shot with two defensive players on the lines.

Procedure

1. The coach sets up 15 to 18 feet away on the wing area with the ball.
2. Two offensive players set up four to five steps outside the lane, opposite the coach.
3. Two defensive players assume good help-side defensive positions.
4. When the coach is satisfied with the position, offense takes the shot.
5. Defense must find their players and keep them from getting pushed out of position.
6. If defense gets the rebound, they rotate to offense. Offense goes to the back of the line. If offense gets the rebound, they score. Defense must sprint to the other end, then to the back of the line.

Coaching Points

- Teach players to work from the off-ball defensive positions they would be in during a game.
- Teach defensive players to find their blockout responsibility, initiate the contact, then go to the ball.

Variations

- The coach can change the shot distances and angles to vary the rebounds.
- Substitute springs with push-ups, jumps, or bleacher sprints.
- Make it competitive by keeping score.

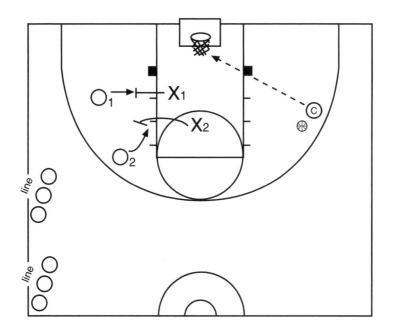

Hamburger Drill

Coach Marnie Daiko
School Cornell University

Purpose
To teach hustle, aggressive, hard-nosed rebounding.

Organization
Three teams of three or four players in lines at the top of the key, right and left wings.

Procedure
1. Teams A, B, and C will send out their number one players (the player who is first in line). They will all meet in the key. The coach will shoot the ball. On a miss or make all players fight to get the ball. Whoever comes up with the ball is the offensive player and looks to score, using not more than five dribbles. The other two players are playing defense on the ball (the player who has the ball).

2. If the player scores, all fight to get the ball out of the net. Whoever comes up with the ball passes to her team to reset the drill. This player is now the offensive post player and looks to receive a pass from her teammate.

3. On any missed shot, the ball is still alive and all three players battle for the rebound. After rebounding, the player with the ball looks for an automatic put back or has five dribbles to score.

4. Once any player scores two baskets she is out of the drill. She goes to the end of her team's line, and the next player in that line comes into the drill.

5. The first team in which each player scores two baskets wins the drill. With four players on four teams, each team needs eight baskets to win.

Coaching Points
- Discourage fouling.
- Encourage aggressive rebounding.

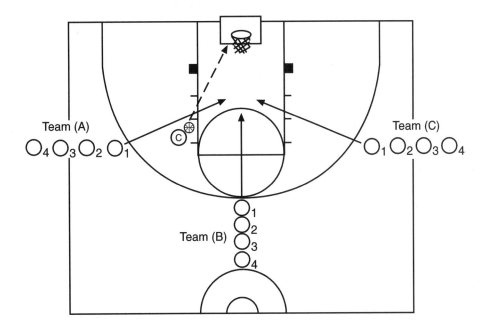

Three on Three Block Out Transition

Carol Hammerle
Northern Illinois University

Purpose
To focus on blocking out, rebounding, and transition of defense to offense.

Organization
Three offensive players, three defensive players, and a coach with a ball. Play begins at half court with a block out; then add full court for transition work for both defense and offense.

Procedure
1. Offensive players begin setting screens for one another.
2. Defensive players adjust their positions to offensive movement and ball location.
3. The coach shoots and defense executes a block out.
4. Once defense obtains a rebound, they become the offense, going to the opposite basket.
5. The offense converting to defense must transition and get back.
6. The drill ends with a basket scored or the defense making a stop and converting to offense.

Coaching Points
- Initially, defensive players need *vision* and *communication* to know a shot has been taken.
- Defense must complete play with rebounding before going on offense.
- Teach defensive transition principles, including defending the basket, stopping the ball, and rotating to another player.
- Three on three is the ultimate test of defense. All defensive concepts are used in a three-on-three full-court situation.

Variation
- Start the drill three on three with an offensive player shooting the ball instead of a coach.

1

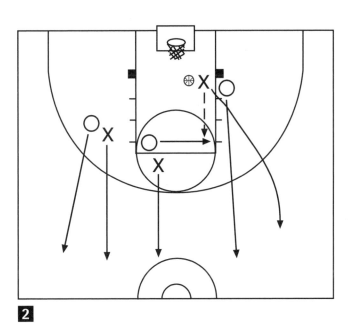

2

Winners and Losers

Coach Kris Huffman
School Depaw University

Purpose
To practice offensive and defensive rebounding technique. This drill also works on closing out and finishing under pressure.

Organization
Twelve players, one ball, four lines formed at the four corners of the lane (offensive players at elbows, defensive players start on baseline).

Procedure
1. The coach passes to either offensive line. Both defenders close out.
2. The player with the ball must shoot upon receiving the ball.
3. The defenders box out. The drill becomes live two on two at this point.
4. Both offensive and defensive players are trying to rebound the shot, made or missed, and *score.*
5. The pair that scores wins (the first shot from the elbow doesn't count).
6. The winning pair gets in the defensive line on the baseline; the nonwinning pair lines up at the top of the key. After five minutes, the players who are lined up at the top of the key must run.

Coaching Points
- Both defenders must close out with the inside hand and foot up.
- Defenders must establish contact and gain good rebounding position.
- The shooter must go up strong and finish inside.

Variations
- When the drill becomes live two on two, limit the number of dribbles allowed.
- Vary the starting position of the offensive lines—midpost, wings, three-point shot, and so on.
- Allow the offensive player to drive after receiving the pass from the coach. This will force a good closeout.

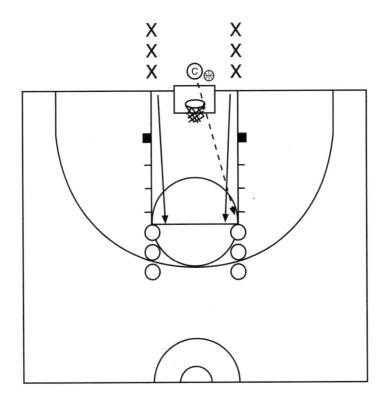

Two on Two

Coach Yvonne Kauffman
School Elizabethtown College

Purpose
To work on defense against the screen and roll and on defensive *rebounding*.

Organization
One ball, two players (one at either side of the foul line), two lines of players behind the baseline.

Procedure
1. X_1 rolls the ball out to either O_1 or O_2 (see diagram 1).
2. X_1 and X_2 close out and play defense on O_1 and O_2 (see diagram 2).
3. O_1 and O_2 try to screen and roll (see diagram 3).
4. X_1 and X_2 play defense while offense tries to score.
5. Play out the point until defense steals the ball, gets the rebound, or offense scores.
6. If defense gets the ball, they go to offense and offense goes behind the defensive line on the baseline.

Coaching Points
- Teach players how you want them to defend the screen and roll.
- Emphasize the box out on the shot.

Variation
- O_1 and O_2 stay on offense. If offense scores, X_1 and X_2 must sprint to the other end and back.

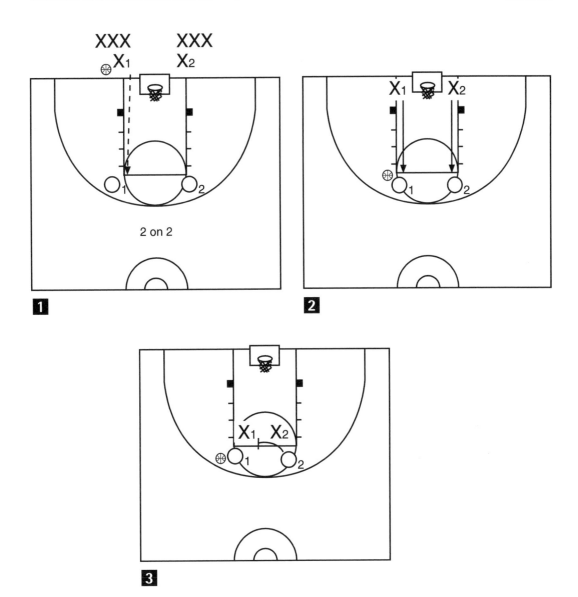

2 on 2

1

2

3

Triangle Box Outs

Coach Wendy Larry
School Old Dominion University

Purpose
To practice rotation on box outs when there is a front in the post.

Organization
Six players per basket: one coach, one ball, three players on both offense and defense. One offensive player is at the ball-side post. One offensive player is at the top of the key. The last offensive player is at the off-ball wing. Defense matches up, fronting the post.

Procedure
1. The coach will bounce the ball once. Every time the coach bounces the ball, there is a rotation.
2. To rotate, the off-ball defender rotates to the post defender's spot. The post defender moves to the top of the key, and the defender at the top of the key moves to the off-ball defense. Offense does not move.
3. The coach bounces the ball three times maximum, then shoots. Because there is no on-ball defense, coach will yell, "shot."
4. When there is a shot, there is a rotation, but instead of getting in defensive positions, defenders are boxing out the offensive player they are rotating to. Offense crashes the boards hard.

Coaching Points
- The defense must get three rebounds in a row to change to offense.
- The defense must be in good help-defense position—no cheating!
- Teamwork is key. If one person forgets to rotate, someone will be wide open for a rebound and put back.

Variations
- Add another offensive and defensive player.
- Change the number of rebounds necessary for defense to change to offense.

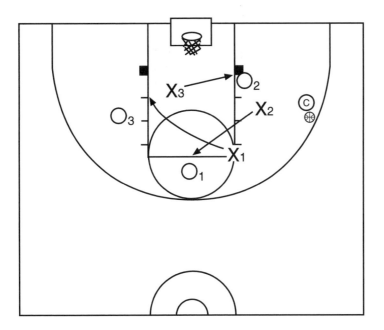

Triangle Rebounding Drill

Coach June Olkowski
School Northwestern University

Purpose
To show players how to rebound out of help position.

Organization
Three offensive players, three defensive players, half court.

Procedure
1. Align the offense on ball-side block, high post, and weak-side block. Add defense.
2. Have the defense slide (clockwise or counterclockwise) to the next offensive player. Defensive assignments will change (post defense, one pass away, and help).
3. The coach shoots the ball; defense and offense react. The drill ends with a score or a rebound.

Coaching Points
- Work on rebounding in gamelike situations, as well as post defense, denial, and weak-side help.
- Defense must communicate.

Variations
- Pass to any offensive player.
- Have defense go in transition on the rebound to work on the outlet pass.

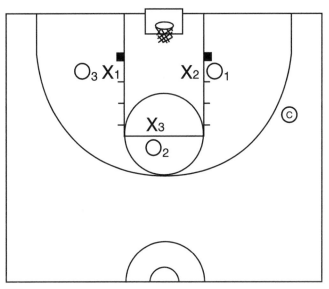

1

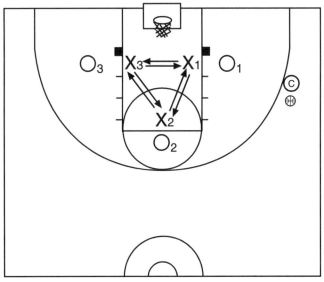

2

Help-Side Rebounding

Coach June Olkowski
School Northwestern University

Purpose
To make contact on block out from a help-side position.

Organization
Four players (two offense and two defense), one ball. Two lines feed from the baseline, with the coach under the basket.

Procedure
1. Offense is facing the coach ready to receive the ball.
2. The defensive players have their backs to the coach at the baseline ready to react.
3. The coach rolls the ball to either wing; the closest defense closes out on the shooter.
4. The opposite defense blocks out for a weak-side rebound.
5. Rotate defense to offense, and move offense out.

Coaching Points
- Close out in a low stance to the ball with hands up.
- Help-side defense, step to the player and make contact.

Variation
- One on one, two on two, three on three.

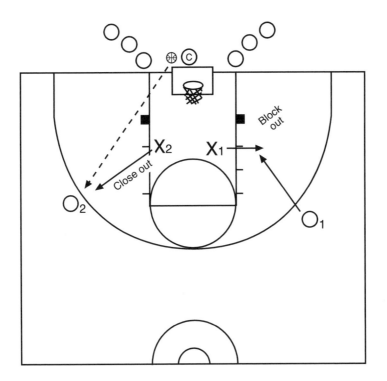

Circle Rebounding

Coach June Olkowski
School Northwestern University

Purpose

To make and maintain contact during block out, so offense cannot touch the ball.

Organization

Two offensive and two defensive players, one ball, a towel, a coach shooting the ball.

Procedure

1. Start with two defensive players; a defender with one ball is on the floor.
2. On command of the shot, defense makes contact and turns to block out, and offense pursues the ball.
3. Maintain contact for specified time (e.g., two or three seconds). The drills end when defense successfully keeps offense away from ball or offense touches the ball. Reward accordingly.

Coaching Points

- Have defense hold a towel above her head so contact with offense is with the lower body.
- If offense is quicker than defense, it's OK to face guard.

Variations

- Add more players.
- Offense may move around.
- Whoever grabs the ball can go to a scorer.

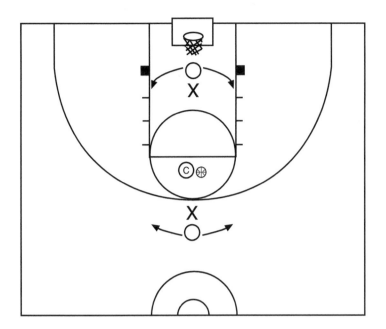

O-D-O Drill
(Offense-Defense-Out)

Coach Amy Ruley
School North Dakota State University

Purpose
To teach defending from a help position, the defender will close out and block out shooters and nonshooters consecutively for a one-minute period (alternating between diagrams 1 and 2).

Organization
Two balls for coach, two lines for offensive shooters and nonshooters, and one defender.

Procedure
1. The coach shoots the ball as the defender is in a help position. The offensive player crashes the boards while the defender takes one or two hard steps to meet the player to block out (see diagram 1).
2. The coach skip passes to an offensive player as the defender is in a help position. The defender sprints and closes out at arm's length from her player. The defender contests the shot and blocks out (see diagram 2).

Coaching Points
- Close out (defensive stance, high hands, low hips).
- Contest shot (keep a hand in the player's face; stay low when adding shot fakes).
- Block out (make contact). Use forward or reverse pivot depending on the player's position.
- Communicate. Shout "Shot!"
- Balance (keep a low center of gravity, with hands up; be ready to jump and go after the ball).

Variations
- Add offensive player movement with and without the ball.
- Add another defender—down screens, cross screens.
- One on one or two on two live.

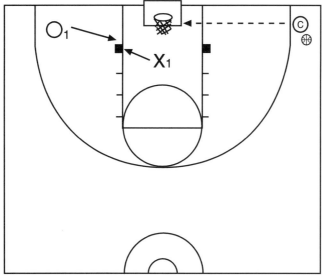

1

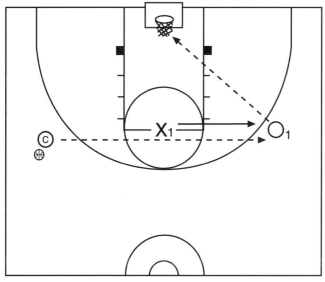

2

41 Four-Player Shell Protection

Coach Amy Ruley
School North Dakota State University

Purpose
To teach defensive team rebounding, focusing on closing out, contesting shots, and blocking out. The defensive team must grab three consecutive team rebounds.

Organization
One coach with the ball underneath the basket, four offensive players spread out in different shooting areas, four defensive players facing their players in a defensive stance.

Procedure
1. The coach bounces the ball on the floor and passes to an offensive player. The defensive team slaps the floor, shouts "Defense," then sprints to a closeout stance to contest the shooter or nonshooter.
2. The offensive rebounds are live. The defensive team rebounds the outlet to a guard on the same side of the floor.
3. The defensive team stays until their team achieves three consecutive rebounds. Rotation is offense to defense, defense out, with a new team entering on offense.

Coaching Points
- See the player and see the ball.
- Block out using a reverse or the forward pivot, depending on player positioning.
- Anticipate the location of the rebound.
- Be physical—make contact to hold your position.
- Focus on protection first, possession second.

Variations
- The shooter may use a dribble.
- Defensive rebounds are live; make the conversion into a fast break.
- Four on four live (cross screens, down screens, screen on the ball).

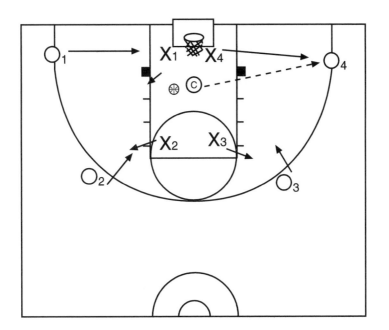

Two Players Defend and Rebound

Coach Pat Summitt
School University of Tennessee

Purpose
To teach communication on defense and refine defensive players' reactions to the ball when offense takes a shot.

Organization
All players, one ball, two lines of players on opposite wing positions.

Procedure
1. Start on either wing; offense has the ball (see diagram 1).
2. The defensive player opposite the ball calls for help.
3. The defensive player on the ball side tries to keep the ball on the sideline.
4. The offensive player can take only two dribbles, then passes across to a teammate who tries to score.
5. Defenders contest the shot, block out offensive players, and follow the shot (see diagram 2).

Coaching Points
- Start with the ball in the wing player's hand. Look to drive to the baseline.
- Allow the crosscourt pass.
- Stress both offensive and defensive rebounding.

Variation
- You can increase the competitiveness by starting with a pass to the wing having the defender in denial position. Don't allow the crosscourt pass, but still challenge the defense to try it.

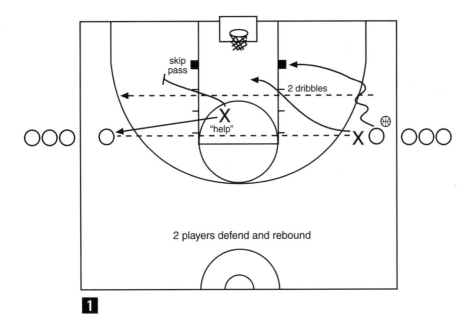

1

2 players defend and rebound

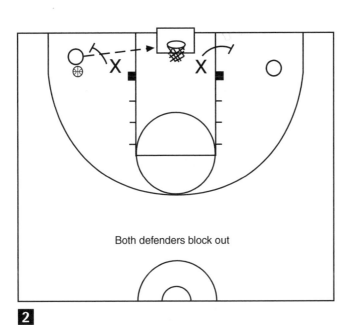

2

Both defenders block out

PERIMETER DRILLS

The pressure of a Tennessee or Southwest Missouri State might give some coaches or players nightmares. The players on those teams know they have worked long and hard to make their opponents' nights sleepless. The hard work, unselfishness, and effort that they must expend to apply full-court unrelenting perimeter pressure are remarkable. Not many individuals, much less teams, can make that kind of commitment successfully over time.

Nonetheless, unrelenting full-court perimeter pressure is the cornerstone of many championship teams. The fear they impose exudes an attitude of confidence and total team commitment, in which everyone will sacrifice to make the play or control the tempo. Many of these teams are made up of average to above average players with extraordinary enthusiasm and commitment to unselfish play.

Regardless of your defensive philosophy, do your players know how to deny entry passes, cut cutters, and influence dribblers? If you'd like help reinforcing their skills, refocusing their abilities, or pushing their limits, read on and see what some of the best coaches in the country are doing to make sure their players are sleeping soundly at night!

Three-Line Closeout

Coach Ceal Barry
School University of Colorado

Purpose
To teach defenders, from help-side position, to quickly approach and defend the shooter who has just received the ball.

Organization
The coach is at the top of the key with a ball; six players stand along the three-point line with the four closest to the baseline each holding a ball. Three players (defenders) line up in help-side position in the middle of the lane. The remaining players wait on the baseline ready to come in as defense. Rotate defense to offense and offense to the line on the baseline. Next three defenders in line come onto court and stutter feet.

Procedure
1. Three defenders stutter feet from the help-side position.
2. As the coach passes the ball to the wing, each defender quickly closes out to her player.
3. The offensive player pivots with the ball protected, while the defender mirrors the ball and calls, "Ball."
4. The coach blows the whistle and the player on the wing passes the ball back to the coach.
5. Three defenders become offense; three offensive players go to the end of the defensive line; three new defenders come in and stutter feet.
6. The coach passes to the opposite wing and repeats the drill.

Coaching Points
- Quickly get out to the ball while under control.
- Hold both hands up when closing out.
- Mirror the ball.

Variation
- Use coaches and managers as offensive players and have the team play only defense.

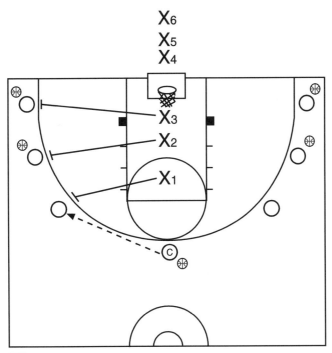

1

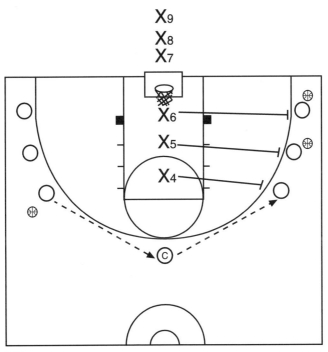

2

Closeout

Coach Nikki Caldwell
School University of Virginia

Purpose
To help players defend penetration and get to the help-side position.

Organization
Four players, offense and defense on the perimeter, one ball, two lines, (a line on each wing). The rotation moves offense to defense, and new offense comes in. The coach will be a passer at the top with a ball.

Procedure
1. The defense will deny passes to the wings.
2. As the coach passes to one side, the weak-side defender will rotate into help-side defense. Make sure players are in the middle of the lane (see diagram 1).
3. To reverse the ball, either pass to the coach then reverse the ball, or use a skip pass to the opposite wing.
4. The defense will move from help-side defense to on-ball defense (see diagram 2).
5. Make sure the players come out in a stance with their feet moving, to force the offense to the baseline. Do not let the offensive player come back to the middle.
6. The other defender will now become the help-side defense.

Coaching Points
- The player must get off to the help side.
- When the ball is reversed, come out to defend in a defensive stance, with feet moving.
- Have active hands, and force the offensive player to the baseline. Keep penetration out of the middle of the court.

Variation
- Once the weak-side player recovers, let the defender get beat and have the help-side defender rotate over and take the charge.

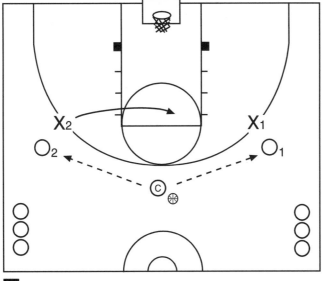

1

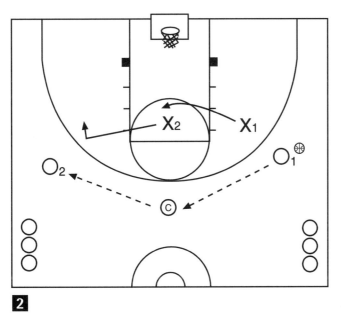

2

Doubling On-Ball Screens

Coach Elaine Elliott
School University of Utah

Purpose

To improve players' footwork and on-ball screen doubling abilities.

Organization

Four players (two offensive, two defensive), one coach, and one ball.

Procedure

1. O_1 starts with the ball on the right wing. O_5 starts at the block with defense. The coach is at the top of the key.

2. O_5 comes out and sets an on-ball screen on the sideline side of X_1.

3. When the screen is set, X_1 immediately shifts to force O_1 to her right to use the screen. X_1 should prevent O_1 from dribbling to the middle of the court. X_2 moves above O_5, into a hedge position, to prevent O_1 from coming off O_5's screen. X_5 should be close enough to O_5 so their feet are either touching or overlapping a little (see diagram 1).

4. O_1 tries to dribble to the basket, either to the left or to the right. X_1 and X_5 should prevent this by closing in on player O_1, so her only options are to back dribble or to pick up the ball (see diagram 2).

5. The drill ends when player O_1 is able to beat the trap and get to the basket or when player O_1 picks up the ball. When a dead ball occurs, defenders close in and prevent a pass out of double team. Go until there is a pass to the coach or a dead ball five-second count.

Coaching Points

- Defenders must keep their knees bent, seat down, and shuffle their feet when trapping. Do not reach to get the ball.

- The defenders' priority should be to prevent getting split by the offensive player. They should also not let the offensive player get to the middle of the court and instead, force her into the sideline.

Variations

- Do this drill on both sides of the floor and on both ends if you have enough players.

- The offensive player, O_1, may be a coach so she can control offensive movement. For example, you can have the coach take only four or five back dribbles, then pick up for a dead ball.

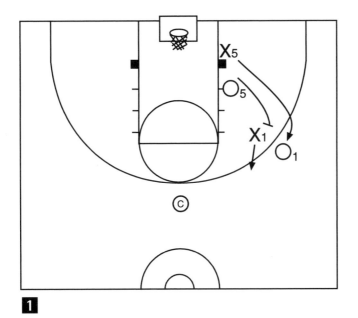

1

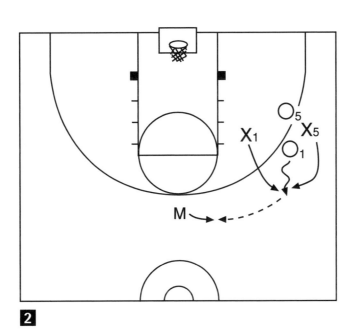

2

Coach Elaine Elliott
School University of Utah

Purpose

To teach defenders on- and off-ball defensive positions.

Organization

Two offensive players, two defensive players, two coaches, one ball, and a 30-second shot clock.

Procedure

1. One offensive player is at each wing position. Two coaches are at the top of the key with a ball. One defender is on each offensive wing player.

2. Position the defense according to where the ball begins. In diagram 1, the ball is with the left coach. Therefore, the left wing defense is one pass away in deny stance. The other defender is two passes away, so she should be in an open pistol stance, one foot in the lane and pointing to see both her player and the ball.

3. Defense shifts position when offense passes the ball. If the ball is passed to the right coach, X_1 will move over into an open stance, one foot in the lane, because she is now two passes away. X_2 will sprint into a denial stance on her offensive player, because she is one pass away (see diagram 2).

4. If offense then passes the ball to the O_2 player, the defender must move from denial to on-ball stance. The other defender must sprint to the middle of the lane, still in pistol stance (see diagram 3).

5. Offense passes the ball around the perimeter for the duration of the 30-second shot clock.

Coaching Points

- Emphasize defenders moving when the ball is in the *air*, not after the pass is made.

- Defenders must stay low in their stances and be able to see their players and the ball.

- Have the offensive players and managers hold the ball for a few seconds so defense can adjust.

Variations

- Offensive players may drive to the basket or shoot on the catch. Defenders must prevent the drive or contest the shot, block out, and rebound.

- Add skip passes for defensive closeout work.

- Add more time to the drill for conditioning.

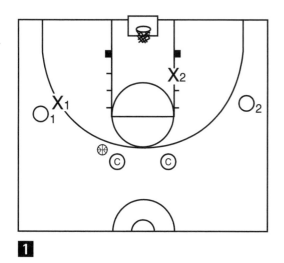

1

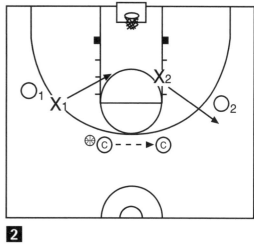

2

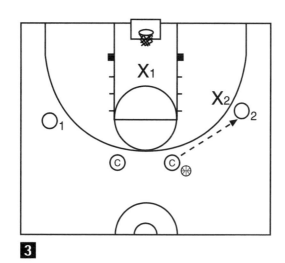

3

Help and Recover Drill

Coach Nancy Fahey
School Washington University

Purpose
To work on help and recover out of a three-player half-court weave.

Organization
Three offensive players, one ball.

Procedure
1. Three lines at half court with the basketball in the middle. Run the drill on both half courts at the same time.
2. O_1 passes the ball to player O_2 and cuts behind O_2 as she dribbles to the free throw line area. O_3 sprints to the lane and gets into a defensive stance (see diagram 1).
3. O_2 passes the ball to player O_1 at the wing. O_3 closes out on the ball (O_1). Once O_3 has closed out, O_1 drives the ball hard to the baseline. O_3 must not give up the baseline drive (see diagram 2).
4. Once the ball is stopped, O_3 yells, "Dead," to alert her teammates the ball handler has given up her dribble. O_1 then passes the ball to O_2 at the free throw lane area. O_3 again must close out.
5. O_2 and O_3 play one on one. The drill stops when the offense has scored, or the defense secures a rebound or gets a steal.

Coaching Points
- Develop closeout footwork.
- Stop the baseline drive.
- Don't give up a layup in either position.

1

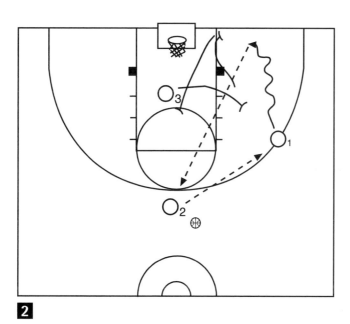

2

Coach Nancy Fahey
School Washington University

Purpose
To reinforce wing denial defense with four or five quick repetitions against offense.

Organization
One offensive player, one defensive player, one coach, one manager, four or five balls.

Procedure
1. Offensive player (O_1) starts at the wing. Defense player (X_1) takes a denial defensive stance.
2. The coach has two basketballs, and the manager is standing next to her with two or three additional basketballs ready to pass to the coach. The coach is on one knee ready to toss the first ball. The remaining players retrieve the basketballs as the defense knocks the basketballs away (see diagram 1).
3. The coach bounces the ball to start the drill. On the bounce, O_1 starts backdoor and pops back out to the wing. X_1 slides down and back to the wing. On a toss from the coach, X_1 knocks the ball down using correct footwork and correct hand movements.
4. O_1 makes three or four cuts; X_1 knocks the ball down each time. On the fourth ball, O_1 cuts to the opposite wing. The coach passes the ball to O_1 at the opposite wing. O_1 and X_1 play one on one until O_1 scores or X_1 secures the ball on a steal or rebound (see diagram 2).

Coaching Points
- Use appropriate footwork and denial hand with the palm to the coach.
- Knock the ball rather than turning to catch it.

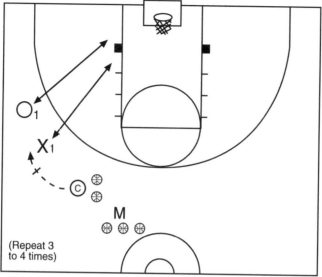

1

(Repeat 3 to 4 times)

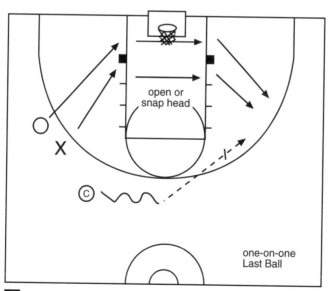

open or snap head

one-on-one Last Ball

2

Cutting Loose

Coach Theresa Grentz
School University of Illinois

Purpose
To improve defensive post play.

Organization
One offensive player, one defensive player, and one coach.

Procedure
1. Each offensive and defensive player begin the drill at the top of the key.
2. The coach takes a position in the wing area on the same side of the floor.
3. The drill begins with the offensive player passing the ball to the coach, then cutting down the lane for the return pass from the coach. The offense makes cuts within the lane in an attempt to get open.
4. The defense must defend all possible cuts by the offense.

Coaching Points
- The defense must make a decision on whether to front, play ball-side defense, or overplay pressure on the ball side.
- Emphasize maintaining correct position on defense in the post.

Variation
- Add weak-side help for defensive players.

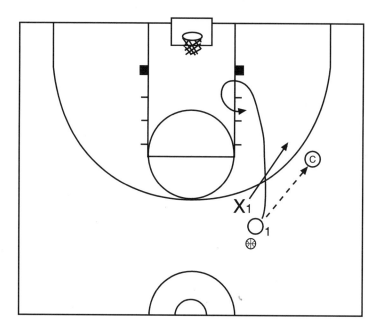

Shell Defense

Coach Theresa Grentz
School University of Illinois

Purpose
To teach basic perimeter defense.

Organization
Four offense and four defense (two offense on both sides of the top of the key and the other two offense in the low wing area), defense matches up accordingly.

Procedure
1. Either guard may start with the ball. The defensive player pressures the ball.
2. The players one pass away from the ball maintain one hand in the passing lane at all times.
3. Offense moves to present the best possible passing target.
4. As the ball changes position, the defensive players adjusts their positions accordingly.

Coaching Points
- The player guarding the ball *always* applies pressure to minimize the offense's ability to see the passing lanes.
- Defensive players one pass away should deny the pass.
- The defender who is more than one pass away should be prepared to help on penetration to the basket.
- Players should see both the ball and their offensive player at all times.

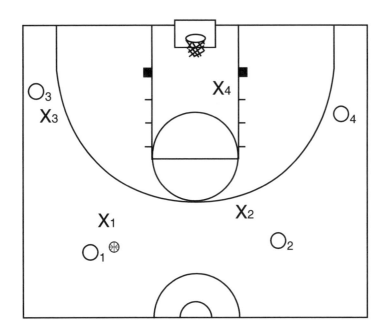

Timed Shell

Coach Kris Huffman
School Depaw University

Purpose
To help establish team defense concepts. This drill includes ball side, help side, hedging, moving with each pass, and finishes with the rebound.

Organization
Twelve players, one ball, four lines, a manager to time the drill. Four offensive players line up around the three-point line with four defenders.

Procedure
1. Any offensive player may start with the ball. Defenders assume proper positioning.
2. The offense passes the ball around the perimeter; the defense adjusts with each pass.
3. The manager blows the whistle after 20 seconds. Offense becomes defense, and defense chooses a different line.
4. Each group plays defense for one or two sequences. Then add dribble penetration to the drill.
5. The defense must help and recover. The offense looks to score.
6. The defense stays on the floor for 20 seconds before rotating.

Coaching Points
- The player guarding the ball should apply pressure.
- Defensive players one pass away should deny; defenders two passes away should be in help-side position.
- On the penetration, the defense should *see* the ball and *stop* the ball.

Variations
- Add the give and go option to make the defense work on jumping to the ball.
- Add the weak-side flash.
- Have all the defenders begin in the lane. The coach can pass the ball to any offensive player. The defense must quickly establish a good defensive position relative to the ball.

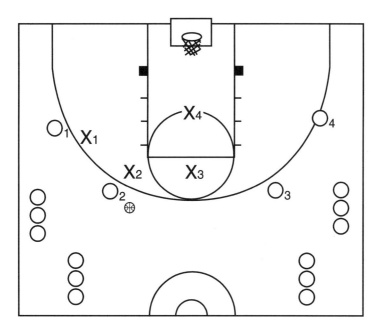

One-on-One Force Corner

Coach Kris Huffman
School Depaw University

Purpose
To influence the offense to the corner keeping the ball out of the middle of the floor and not allowing ball reversal.

Organization
One ball, one line, one defender, a coach with the ball opposite the line of players.

Procedure
1. The drill begins with a skip pass from the coach to the offensive player on the wing.
2. The defender must adjust from help side to defending the ball with a good closeout.
3. The drill is now one on one.
4. The defender attempts to influence the ball to the corner and protect the middle.
5. The drill ends with the made basket or the rebound and outlet pass.

Coaching Points
- The defender must close out in a stance with the inside foot and hand up.
- The defender must not give up an open lane to the basket when trying to keep the offensive player out of the middle. Angle the feet to the corner, not the baseline.

Variation
- Limit the number of dribbles allowed by the offense.

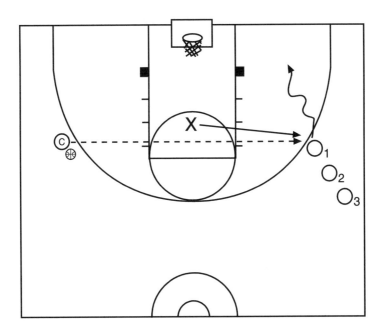

Wing Denial

Coach Wendy Larry
School Old Dominion University

Purpose

To practice perimeter defensive positioning when one pass away and denying the ball. This drill also works on help-side positioning when the ball is on the opposite side of the court.

Organization

Four players (two offense, two defense), two coaches, one ball. The two coaches are at the top of the key; one offense and one defense are on each wing.

Procedure

1. One coach starts with the ball. The offense on her side attempts to get open while the defense denies.
2. Off-ball defense is two passes away and should be in help position.
3. If offense gets open and receives the ball, they play two on two until offense scores or defense gets the ball.
4. If offense on that side of the court *cannot* get open, one coach passes to the other coach and they repeat steps 1 through 3.
5. If defense is successful in denying offense the ball four times in a row, switch offense to defense.

Coaching Points

- If the defense is doing a great job of denying, try to get a pass through. Let them get a deflection so they realize the benefits of denying properly.
- In denying, remind the defense to use the proper hand to deflect. Keep good spacing; don't set up too close to the offensive player.
- Allow the offense to make a backdoor cut. Off-ball help should be there!

Variations

- This drill could move quickly if you require only two good denials or if offense scores, defense moves off.
- If you have more than four at the basket, you can rotate players in and out.

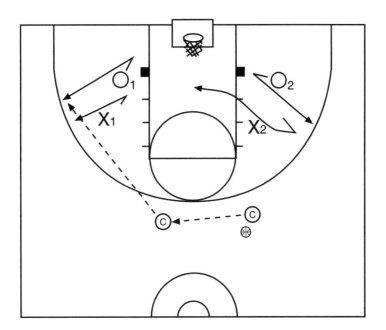

54 Three Players Help and Recover

Coach Pat Summitt
School University of Tennessee

Purpose
To teach ball pressure and help-side recovery.

Organization
Three lines, three offensive players, three defensive players, one ball.

Procedure
1. Start at one end of the floor with the ball in the middle line.
2. The player with the ball can dribble twice, then must pass to either wing.
3. The wing player dribbles twice and passes to the middle or skips to the wing.
4. The first time through, defense allows the passes.
5. The second time through, defense tries to deny passes.
6. When the three offensive players get to the three-point line at the opposite end, they are allowed to attack the basket. It is all-out three on three at that point.

Coaching Points
- Emphasize help and recover to the ball, putting pressure on each pass and dribble.
- Emphasize seeing your player and the ball.
- Don't allow the wing offensive players to get ahead of the ball.

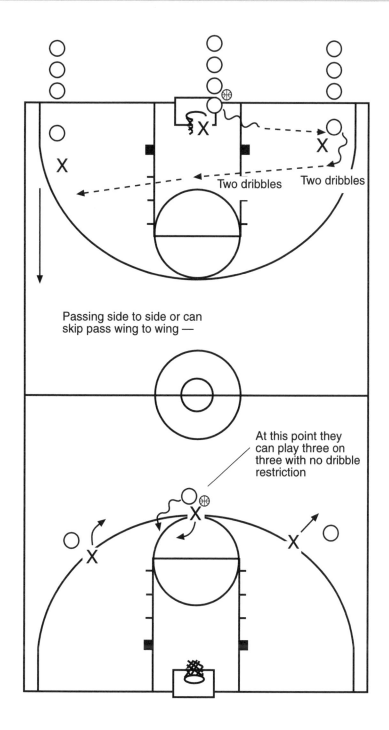

Two dribbles   Two dribbles

Passing side to side or can
skip pass wing to wing —

At this point they
can play three on
three with no dribble
restriction

Deny-Open-Deny

Coach Pat Summitt
School University of Tennessee

Purpose

To teach defenders wing denial and to open in the lane to see the ball and their player.

Organization

Two players (a defensive player and offensive player on the wing); two coaches, each with a ball, one on the right wing and one on the left wing.

Procedure

1. Start with an offensive and defensive player on the left wing.
2. The coach slaps the ball to begin the drill; the defender denies.
3. The offensive player tries to receive the ball at least twice by breaking out to the wing.
4. Then the offensive player goes to the basket, across the lane, and up to the right wing. The defender opens up her stance, fronts the offensive player across the lane, then closes stance and denies the offense cutting to the right wing.

Coaching Points

- Have experienced coaches attempting to pass to the wing.
- Emphasize that the defender should play up the ball line.
- Have defenders react quickly when the offensive player makes her second cut up the wing to receive the ball.

Variation

- On the second attempt to receive the ball on the right wing, the coach attempts a pass that the defender can steal or knock down.

6

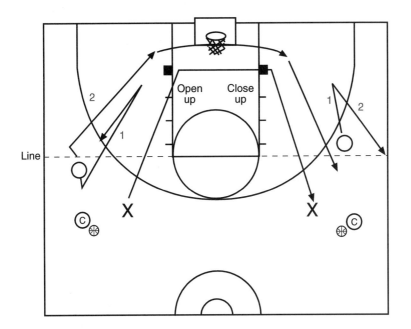

Help and Recover to Three on Three Live

Coach Kay Yow
School North Carolina State University

Purpose
To teach players to help and recover with proper defensive rotations.

Organization
Six players, one coach with two balls, and one manager. Players are positioned in shell defense spots (offense and defense in both corners and offense and defense on the right wing). The coach is on the left wing and the manager is under the basket. Players rotate from offense to defense.

Procedure
1. The ball starts with the coach, who passes to O_1. On the pass, defensive players adjust as shown in diagram 1 (similar to the shell drill).
2. O_1 passes to O_2. Again, the defensive players adjust (see diagram 2).
3. The ball is skip passed back to the coach. The coach drives right, requiring X_1 to help stop penetration. The coach then drives left, requiring X_3 to help stop penetration (see diagram 3).
4. The coach passes to O_3, who penetrates the baseline. For the sake of the drill, X_3 allows O_3 to beat her (see diagram 4).
5. On the penetration, X_2 slides over to help and X_1 drops.
6. O_3 tries to pass across the baseline to O_2. X_1 knocks the ball out of bounds to the manager, and the coach throws a live ball to O_1.
7. Play is live (three on three).

Coaching Points
- Develop good communication between players.
- Give early help, and recover quickly.
- Players helping must have good body position to prevent the coach from getting to the basket. If the body position is open, the coach will have a direct path to the basket.
- Help on the baseline should occur outside the lane line; otherwise it has arrived too late.
- The ball needs to move quickly. This should be a fast-paced, intense drill.

Variation
- Trap the ball handler on the baseline.

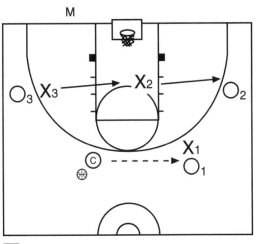

1

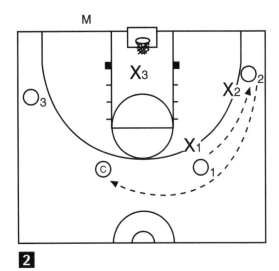

2

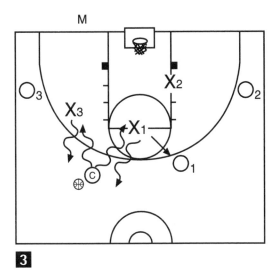

3

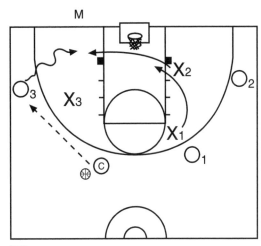

4

5

POST DRILLS

How would you defend a Lisa Leslie? Do you play behind, in front, sag, pressure? It's a tough call. Thankfully, not every post defender is as challenging, yet knowing what your defensive philosophy dictates will guide your players in determining how to best stop a top post player.

As in all defensive approaches, your choice of positioning will impact not only the post players, but also their perimeter teammates. Pressuring intensely on the wings may make passing inside more difficult, and fronting on the low post requires active and conscientious weak-side help. Building your players' confidence and sense of team concept is essential if you are to realize any of your defensive intentions.

Defending Lisa Leslie won't be the challenge of most coaches, but there are certainly other opponents who present a formidable test. Learn from the following coaches what makes their post defenders exceptional, and you'll face any opponent (of any size and stature) with confidence and poise.

Deny the Ball—
Take the Charge

Coach Lisa Bluder
School Drake University

Purpose
To work on denial defense, getting to weak-side position on the pass, helping on the drive, and taking the charge.

Organization
Minimum of three players, one coach, two balls (a manager is helpful).

Procedure
1. The coach begins the drill positioned on one side of the top of the key.
2. Position two offensive players, one on the strong side, one on the weak side.
3. One defensive player denying the pass from the coach on the strong side.
4. The strong-side offensive player tries to get open on one side of the floor. The coach will throw the pass. Defense knocks the pass away and stays in denial position.
5. The coach passes the second ball to the weak side; defense moves on the pass to a good weak-side position.
6. The offensive player with the ball drives. Defense stops the drive and takes the charge outside of the paint.

Coaching Points
- Make sure the defense waits until offense passes the second ball before moving to the weak-side position.
- A manager is helpful to chase the balls that are knocked away.
- Stress good defensive movements.
- Teach players how to take the charge (i.e., how to absorb the contact and land safely).

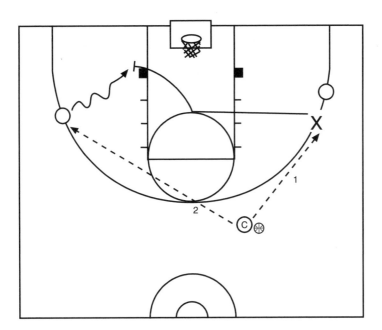

Two on Two in the Post

Coach Lisa Bluder
School Drake University

Purpose
To work on defending the post from the weak-side defense and from the post-to-post screen.

Organization
Two offensive posts; two defensive posts; three coaches, managers, or passers; one ball.

Procedure
1. Put your two offensive and defensive players in the low post area.
2. Use three passers, one at top of the key and one at each wing. Pass the ball from any of these positions into the posts.
3. Offense can post, flash to high post, or screen away.
4. Defense works on proper positioning for post defense.
5. Defense goes to offense, and a new defense steps in on every third possession.

Coaching Points
- Get weak-side posts off their players and moving so they can't be effectively screened.
- Encourage defensive players to talk and communicate on all screens.

Variation
- Have the defensive posts stay on defense until they get a steal or rebound.

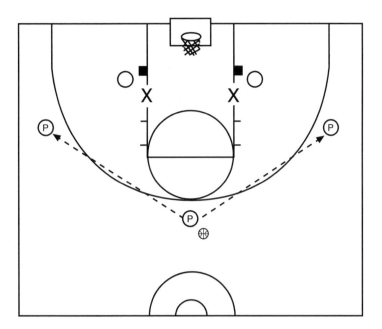

One-on-One Post

Coach Lisa Bluder
School Drake University

Purpose
To work on the reactions of post-offense and post-defense players.

Organization
One offensive and one defensive post, one coach, one ball.

Procedure
1. Two posts are along the lane facing away from the coach near the low block area.
2. The coach has a ball and calls the name of either post.
3. The called player becomes the offense and the other becomes the defense.
4. The offensive player flashes to the strong side to receive the ball, and the defensive player reacts to play defense against her.

Coaching Points
- Develop quick movement to receive a pass, target hand, calling for the ball.
- Use good hustle and footwork on defense to pursue denial of the pass, or use good block out footwork to allow just one shot by the offense.

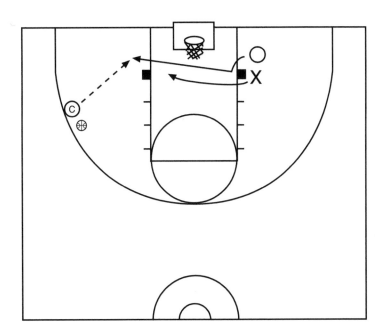

Pit Drill

Coach Lisa Bluder
School Drake University

Purpose
To work on low post defensive footwork and positioning.

Organization
Four passers, one offensman, one defender, one ball.

Procedure
1. Set four passers around the three-point line in typical shell positions.
2. One offensive player and one defender are working at the low post area.
3. The passers will pass the ball around to each other until they can cleanly pass the ball into the post.
4. If post offenseman receives a pass, she makes a move to the basket to score. Defenders box out and outlet to a passer.
5. Continue the drill for one minute. Rotate positions.

Coaching Points
- Don't allow any lob passes because there is no help for the defender.
- Make sure the post offense stays active in trying to get open for the ball.
- Review and teach all possible post-defensive positions, depending on where the ball is.

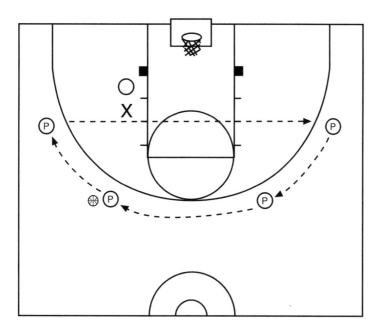

Post Defense

Coach Theresa Grentz
School University of Illinois

Purpose
To prevent the pass into the post player.

Organization
Five players (four offensive and one defensive player), one offensive at the top of the key and one on each wing, one in the low post on either side. Defender assumes a position on the post based on where the ball starts in the drill.

Procedure
1. Players on the perimeter simply pass the ball between themselves.
2. The offensive post player (O_1) is free to move to any position within the free throw lane. The defensive player (X_1) must remain in a good defensive position and attempt to deny the pass into the post.

Coaching Point
- The defensive post player should beat the offense to where she wants to post up.

Variation
- Work on anticipating the post player's cuts and using proper footwork to reestablish good denial defense.

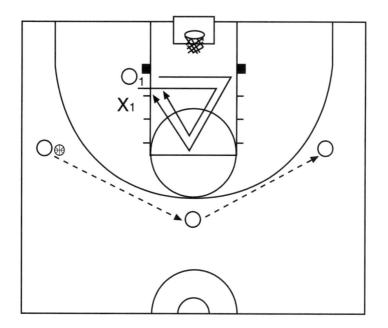

Post Denial

Coach Theresa Grentz
School University of Illinois

Purpose

To teach a denial position pass from a wing and the corner to the post.

Organization

Three offensive and two defensive players (one offensive player on the block, one on the wing, and one in the corner; one defensive player on the wing or corner and the other in the post).

Procedure

1. X_1 pressures the ball when it is either on the wing or in the corner.
2. X_2 denies the pass into the post by playing position defense (depending on where the ball is).
3. If the pass is made into the post, X_1 collapses to assist the post defender.
4. When offense passes the ball out from the post, X_1 goes and pressures the ball.

Coaching Points

- The post defender should step up and deny the entry pass. Players should always have a hand in the passing lane regardless of the ball position. This requires the defense to beat the offense to spots on the floor and see the ball at all times.

- The wing or corner defender *must* attack the ball. She can also double down on the offensive post player to force the ball back out to the wing or the corner.

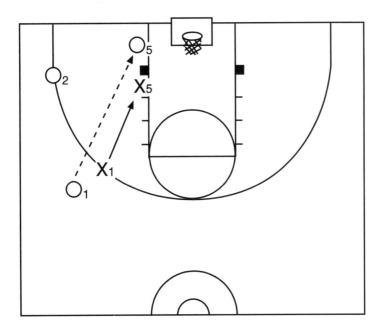

Three-on-Three Cover Down Drill

Coach Jody Runge
School University of Oregon

Purpose

To teach X_5 low post defense. To teach players to defend at different positions on the floor. To teach X_1 and X_2 cover down when the ball goes inside to the low post.

Organization

Players line up as in the diagram. Players rotate offense to defense first. They then rotate positions on the floor. Wing players go to the corner; corner players go to the low post; post players go to the wing.

Procedure

1. The coach starts the drill by passing to the wing O_1.
2. O_1 looks inside for O_5; defenders adjust their positions.
3. O_1 passes to the corner to O_2; defensive players adjust their positions.
4. O_2 passes into low post O_5; defensive players adjust their positions.
5. O_5 can pass the ball back outside and the drill continues. O_5 can shoot the ball and all players are live.

Coaching Points

- The post defender X_5 must spin in front from high to low side as offense passes the ball from wing to corner.
- Defenders X_1 and X_2 must jump to the ball on the pass from wing to corner.
- Defenders X_1 and X_2 must cover down to O_5 when she catches the ball in the low post.

Variations

- You can run the drill with four players on the side.
- You can run the drill on both sides of the floor at the same time.

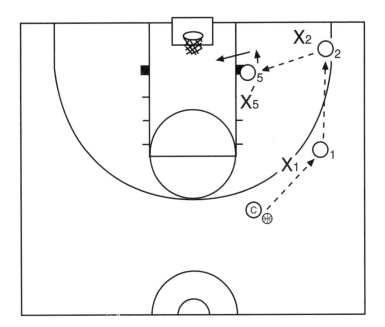

One-on-One Flash-Post Drill

Coach Jody Runge
School University of Oregon

Purpose
To teach post defenders to deny flash-post cuts. To teach hustle in post defense. To teach defense against offensive post moves.

Organization
Players line up as in diagram. Players rotate from O_1 to O_2 to O_3 to X_3 to the end of the line. The first player in line becomes the next O_1. Player O_1 has an extra basketball at her feet.

Procedure
1. Player O_3 flashes toward O_1 with the basketball; defender X_3 denies the flash cut and deflects O_1's pass.
2. Player O_1 picks up the second ball and passes to O_2. O_3 tries to post up on O_2's side of the floor in low post.
3. Defender X_3 must deflect the pass from O_1, then cover O_3, dropping to low post on the ball side.
4. To make the drill competitive X_3 must stop passes to both high flash and low post or must go again.
5. You can run this drill at both ends of the court so all players learn to defend inside.

Coaching Points
- X_3 must deny on the flash cut by moving in her denial stance with her right hand in the passing lane.
- X_3 must sprint to the low post and be in a denial stance with her feet moving.
- Any time the ball is caught, the players go one on one until a shot is taken.

Variations
- To make the drill competitive you can put defenders on O_1 and O_2.
- The drill can become a live three-on-three drill.

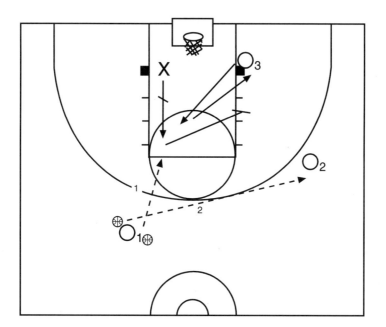

Flash–Post Reaction Drill

Coach Jody Runge
School University of Oregon

Purpose

To teach quick flash-post cuts, quick post-defense reactions, and post-defense stances and body positions.

Organization

Players line up as in diagram. Players can rotate offense to defense, or the defender can make two or more stops to rotate out. The coach has two basketballs. You can use one or two balls in this drill.

Procedure

1. The coach starts the drill by passing to either player on either side of the floor.
2. The player who catches the ball looks for a teammate across from her to flash to the ball. X_5 must deny the flash.
3. The coach then throws the ball to another player on either side.
4. If the coach passes first to a player on the baseline, X_5 must close out and pressure the shot or deny the flash cut.
5. The coach can change the drill up by determining whether players should flash or catch and dive.

Coaching Points

- X_5 must stay in her stance, move her feet, and deny the flash cut. If O_3 catches ball, they go one on one until a shot.
- X_5 must stop the flash cut and knock down the pass, then react to the second pass of the coach.
- A great drill for post players, it makes them quickly react to flash cuts and one-on-one moves.

Variations

- You can use two defensive players and make them work together to deny flash cuts and two-on-two plays.
- To increase the drill's competitiveness, have the defense make two stops before rotating out.

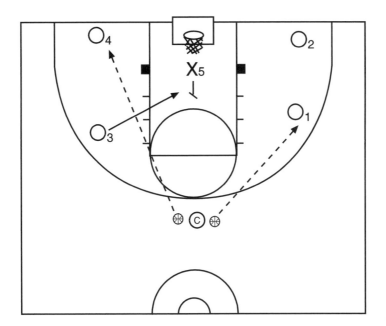

Post-Shot Pressure Drill

Coach Jody Runge
School University of Oregon

Purpose
To teach quick reaction shot pressure and how to pressure shots. To teach post players to have their hands up.

Organization
Players line up as in diagram. Players rotate on the coach's signal. The coach has a basketball and starts the drill with a pass.

Procedure
1. The coach starts the drill with a pass to any of the three offensive players.
2. X_5 must reach to the pass, pressure the shot, and block out the shooter.
3. If O_3, O_4, or O_5 shoots the ball and gets the offensive rebound, she shoots it again until the defender gets the defensive rebound.
4. If X_5 gets the defensive rebound, she tosses the ball back to the coach and gets ready to go again.
5. The coach can then pass to any player again.

Coaching Points
- X_5 must keep her hands up and feet moving to be ready to react.
- The defender must keep her arm straight and wrist back to avoid fouling the shooter.
- The defender must learn to use either hand to pressure the shot.

Variations
- The coach can make passes as quickly or as slowly as possible to give the defender success.
- The coach can keep the defender on defense until she has reacted quickly to pressure shots.

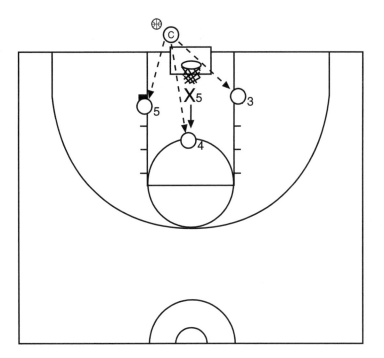

6

TRANSITION DRILLS

With today's game being fast paced and transition oriented, it's no wonder coaches are looking at defensive transition a little differently than 15 years ago. Isn't transition on defense just about getting back and stopping the ball? Well, mostly yes, but in this chapter you'll learn how the top coaches teach their players to not only get back and stop the ball, but also to attempt to dictate and control the offensive team's efforts from the point of turnover.

Essentially coaches aren't satisfied with just getting back; many are attempting to control the offensive tempo (sometimes in the backcourt off the rebound) and cause the ball to turn over again before assuming they are back on defense! Still, there are plenty of teams whose bread and butter rely on sprinting back and protecting the paint. Read on and you'll learn how top coaches are approaching this aspect of the game. Perhaps you'll see some virtue in building their ideas into your winning strategies.

67 Transition D (One on One)

Coach Jane Albright
School University of Wisconsin

Purpose

To make the offensive player turn or change directions and work on full-court one-on-one defense.

Organization

Players paired up by size and speed, then lined up on the baseline, each pair with a ball.

Procedure

1. Both players start at baseline.
2. Defender (X) slides to the manager at the hash mark and slaps the manager's hand.
3. Offense waits until the defender gets to the manager before starting to dribble.
4. The defender is trying to sprint to half court to meet offense.
5. Offense is trying to score at the opposite end of the court.
6. Defense is trying to slow offense by forcing her to change the direction on her dribble.
7. Play out one on one on the opposite end until offense scores or defense gets a rebound or steal.

Coaching Point

- Emphasize staying low on the slide, sprinting hard, and working to make offense change directions with her dribble. This will slow her down and make her easier to defend.

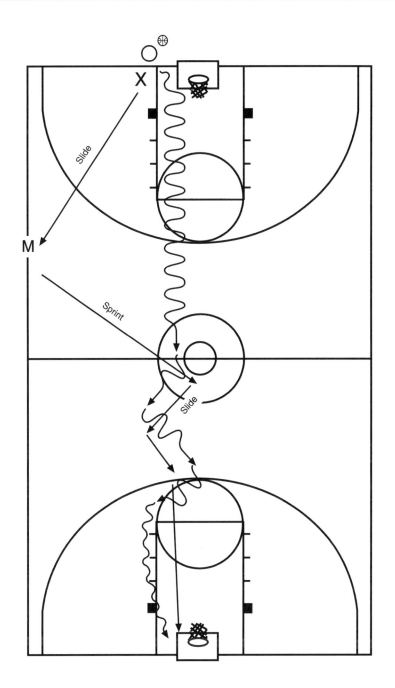

Sideline Attack

Coach Gary Blair
School University of Arkansas

Purpose

To simulate transition defense. To teach good offensive spacing and two-on-two play. It's a fun and competitive drill that conditions without feeling like it is conditioning.

Organization

Two groups, offense and defense. The coach needs two balls to keep the drill moving.

Procedure

1. Four offensive team members space out along the same sideline, baseline to baseline.
2. Two defensive team members start at the free throw lane lines, opposite each other.
3. The coach initiates the drill with a toss to O_1. On the toss, X_1 and X_2 sprint to defend O_3 and O_4 (see diagram 1).
4. O_1 passes to O_2 who passes to O_3, who passes to O_4. O_4 and O_3 then go live against X_1 and X_2.
5. They play two on two until offense scores or defense stops them. Everyone goes off around the outside of the court to the back of their same line (see diagram 2).
6. The next two defenders in line become X_1 and X_2. O_1 and O_2 rotate to O_3 and O_4 spots, and the next two in the offensive line step into O_1 and O_2. The coach tosses the ball to O_1 and repeats the drill.

Coaching Points

- Offense must make strong, quick, crisp passes.
- Defense must sprint to get to defensive position.
- Let each group play offense for a certain number of minutes, then switch.

Variation

- Keep score to make this a fun, competitive drill that is a great way to condition without players even realizing it.

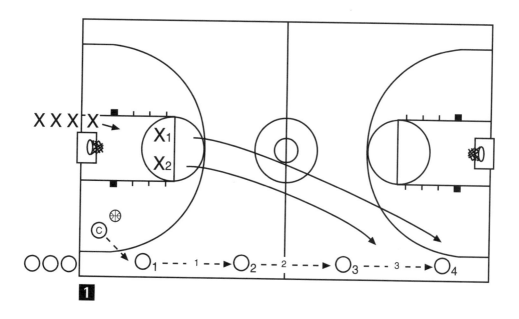

1

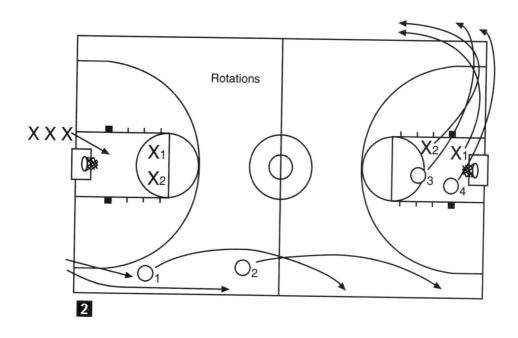

Rotations

2

Two-on-Two Full: On-Ball Screens

Coach Beth Burns
School Ohio State University

Purpose

To work on using on-ball screens for full and half court and inbounding the ball.

Organization

Two offense, two defense (each pair with one guard and one forward), one ball per each group of four.

Procedure

1. All four players are on the court. The coach shoots and makes a layup.

2. The big O_2 gets the ball out of the net, clears the paint, and inbounds to O_1. O_1 breaks to an outlet. X_2 pressures a pass, and X_1 forces an outlet to the ball (see diagram 1).

3. O_1 turns up the court, and O_2 sets the on-ball screen. Have offense set at least one screen in the backcourt (see diagram 2).

4. Set another screen on or around the three-point line of the front court (see diagram 3).

5. Offense attacks the basket to score after the second screen.

6. If offense makes the basket, X_2 clears the paint and inbounds. O_1 and O_2 must react and match up. X_2 will set the on-ball screens.

7. If the missed shot goes to defense or attack, O_1 and O_2 must react and match up. Defense will set the on-ball screens.

Coaching Points

- In the backcourt, X_1 has on-ball pressure, and X_2 stays 12 to 15 feet deeper than the ball, talking loud, "Pick coming." Keep X_2's head on the line of the ball (moving laterally, not forward). X_1 slides behind the screen, then meets the ball on the other side. Repeat this process on any on-ball screen in the backcourt.

- In the frontcourt, have about three feet around the three-point line and in. Do foot to foot with *no switch*. Defense hears the screen and forces the ball to X_2; X_2 steps at the ball (not laterally or behind), keeping her inside hand on O_2's hip. If the hip leaves, you leave because there is no longer a screen (see diagram 4). The goal is to force the ball wide or back with no middle penetration.

Variation

- Players can trap on the balls.

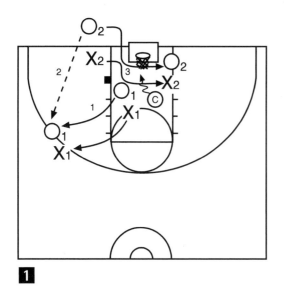

1

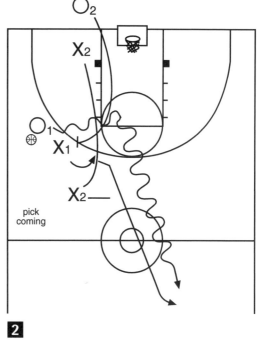

pick
coming

2

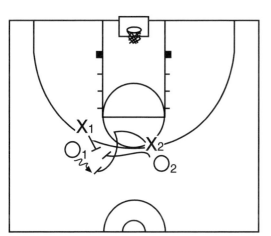

3

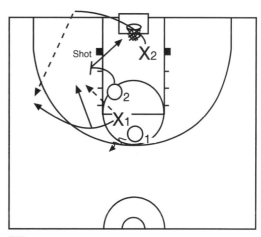

Shot

4

Two-on-Two Full: Basket Positional

Coach Beth Burns
School Ohio State University

Purpose
To teach transition defense, rebounding, defensive positioning, switching on screens.

Organization
Two offense, two defense, one ball for each group of four. Pairs are of similar size, speed, and ability; use a rebound ring to create rebound opportunities.

Procedure
1. X_1 starts with the ball near the baseline and gives it to O_1. Her partner X_2 is in help position (she may or may not be in denial) (see diagram 1).
2. O_1 will penetrate in straight lines; O_2 can sprint out to spread over the floor.
3. As X_1 pressures, O_2 will set the on-ball screen. X_2 must react and call "Switch."
4. The offense takes a shot, but can only get the point by getting the offensive rebound (see diagram 2).
5. When X_1 or X_2 gets possession, she transitions to the other end. O_1 and O_2 must immediately stop the ball and match up. X_1 and X_2 must score (no rebound ring on this basket) to get points.

Coaching Points
- Don't be surprised if the defense gets beat early. This drill forces two players to communicate to be successful.
- Do foot on foot on all switches. Encourage offense to split the screen (ball handler) or slip the screen (screener).
- By having a basket cover up, offense goes hard to glass to score; this makes stopping the transition a challenge.
- Emphasize communication and conditioning.
- Take turns with who gets the ball first.
- Go four to six minutes for 12 players; the winners are those who get the most points.

Variation
- Depending on your goal, you can have at least two on-ball screens or just one screen if pressure dictates it.

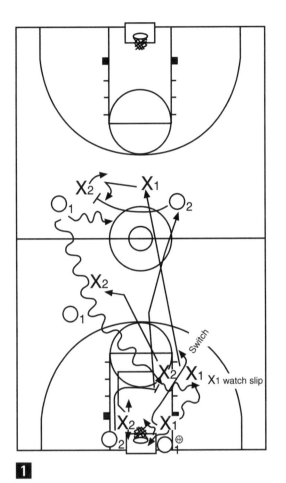

1

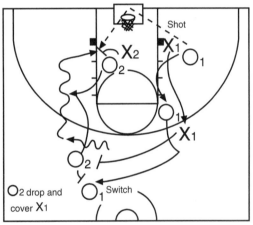

2

71 Full-Court Turn and Cut

Coach Beth Burns
School Ohio State University

Purpose
To play full-court player on-ball defense; to focus on conditioning.

Organization
Players in pairs, one ball for each pair, 30-second shot clock.

Procedure

1. X_1 starts with the ball and starts with her head under the net; she should have her feet set to force the drive to the weak hand. She hands the ball to the offense.
2. Offense tries to attack in straight lines; in the backcourt, X_1 turns the offensive player as many times as possible.
3. As the ball approaches half court, cut the floor and keep the ball on one side.
4. Contest the shot and box out. Partners jog back; pairs are going continuously. The coach calls the shot clock.

Coaching Points

- Use aggression with intelligence (i.e., speed, size of offense).
- Always have one hand in the eye area to distract vision and prevent a full-court pass (see diagram 1).
- Force as many turns as possible in the backcourt.
- Make constant chatter, "ball, ball, ball."
- "Jump back," is what X will say and do if the offense hesitates. The distance is at least the length of the offensive player's first step. Keep the hands up to block a full-court pass (see diagram 1).
- Cut the floor in half; allow no middle penetration (see diagram 2).
- Contest the shot, box out, and play to finish.
- Reward 21 seconds or less left on the clock—defense forced many turns and applied good pressure. If there are 26 or 27 seconds remaining, the ball came up the court too quickly.

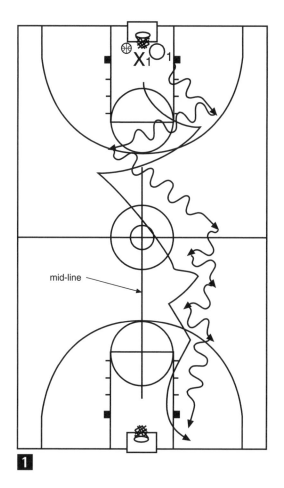

1

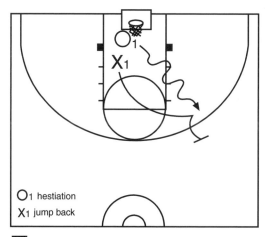

O₁ hestiation
X₁ jump back

2

Five on Four Plus One

Coach Bonnie Henrickson
School Virginia Tech

Purpose
To learn how to stop the ball in transition and communicate rotations once the ball gets to half court.

Organization
Five offensive players, five defensive players, one ball.

Procedure
1. The five offensive players line up on the baseline; the five defensive players line up on the free throw line (see diagram 1).
2. The coach throws the ball to an offensive player. The defensive player standing across from the receiver runs to touch the baseline she's facing.
3. Ahead of time, the coach dictates which defender stops the ball and which defender gets back to protect the basket.
4. In diagram 2, X_1 is protecting the basket; X_2 is stopping the ball.
5. X_4 sprints the full length of the floor to make it five on five.
6. The offense tries to get a high-percentage shot before it becomes five on five.

Coaching Points
- Stop play opposite the three-point line to check the defensive position.
- Emphasize communication—players must talk and find their matchups.
- Have the defense line up in different positions, not always posts across from posts and guards across from guards. This will give you some mismatches.

Variation
- Give a time limit to score (e.g., the offense has to take a shot in 12 seconds).

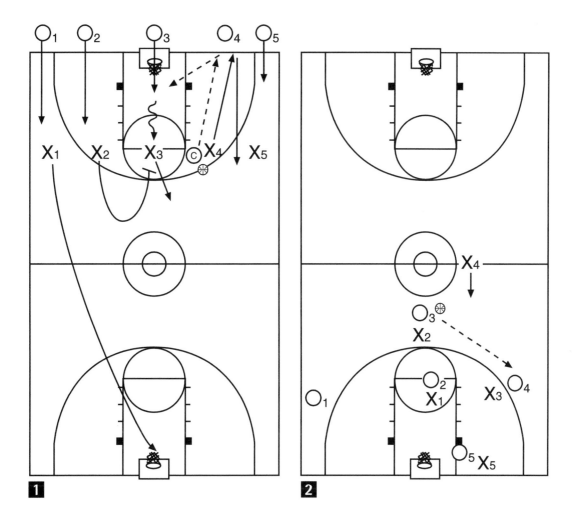

1

2

VT Release

Coach Bonnie Henrickson
School Virginia Tech

Purpose
To emphasize the fullback position (the player assigned to protect the basket) in defensive transition.

Organization
Six offensive players, five defensive players, one ball.

Procedure
1. Five players execute your offense or freelance (depending on what you want).
2. On your command, a player takes a shot.
3. The rebounder outlets to the point guard and goes out of the drill to make it five on five on the other end.
4. The sixth offensive player at half court releases (flys) on your command to force the fullback to get back on the shot.
5. In the diagram, O_1 is now the fullback, and O_2 stops the ball.

Coaching Points
- Let the outlet throw the ball to the players flying if they are open.
- Stop to check the defensive position of all five players.

Variations
- You can start this drill initially with four on four and build to five on five.
- Add a bubble on the basket of five on five to work on rebounding.
- Put a time limit on the shot attempt.

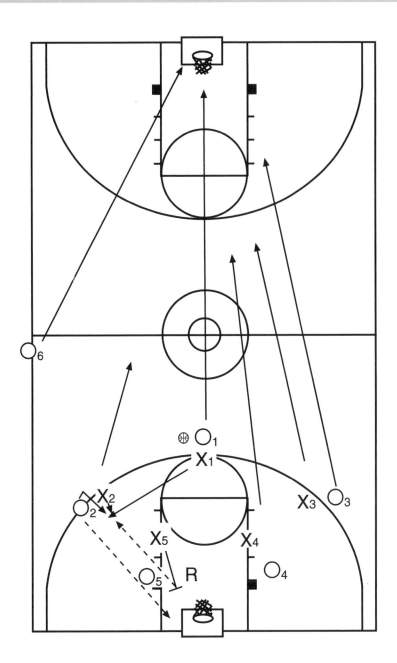

Three on Two Plus One

Coach Bonnie Henrickson
School Virginia Tech

Purpose

To learn the concept of a tandem defensive set; to learn how to stop penetration and protect the basket on defense, even when outnumbered.

Organization

Three offensive players, three defensive players, one coach, and one ball.

Procedure

1. Three offensive players line up on the baseline; three defensive players are on the free throw line (see diagram 1).
2. The coach throws the ball to any offensive player.
3. The defensive player standing across from the receiver sprints to touch the baseline she's facing.
4. X_2 and X_3 sprint back and get into a tandem defensive position. In diagram 2, X_2 takes the first pass and X_3 drops to the baseline. X_1 sprints back to guard O_2.

Coaching Points

- Make sure X_3 drops below O_3 and is at basket level for help.
- Emphasize communication.

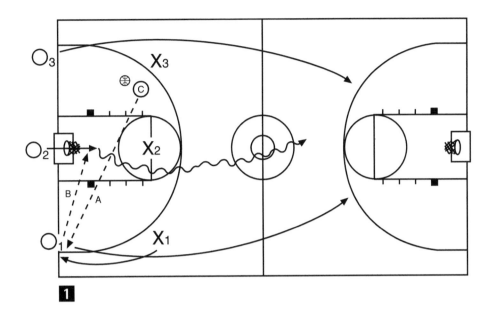

1

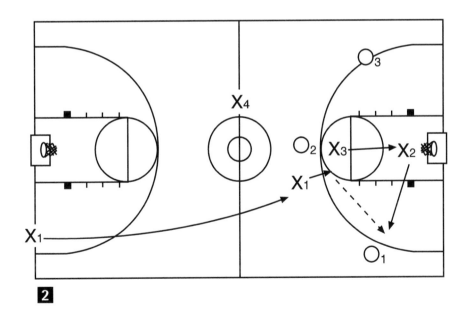

2

Three-on-Three Defensive Transition

Coach Wendy Larry
School Old Dominion University

Purpose

To improve defensive communication and teamwork against a fast break. This is also an excellent conditioning drill.

Organization

Two teams, one ball. One team lines up on a hash mark. The other team lines up at the hash mark on the opposite side and opposite half of the court. Run the clock for five to seven minutes.

Procedure

1. Three players from each team step onto the court. The three that are on their own side of the floor are on defense.

2. These players play three on three until offense scores or defense gets the ball (rebound or steal).

3. If offense scores or defense gets the ball, defense now becomes offense.

4. The defender who steals or rebounds (on a make or a miss) outlets the ball to her teammate who is next in line, then goes to the end of the line (see diagram 1).

5. The outlet and two other defenders now attack the three offensive players on a three-on-three fast break (see diagram 2).

6. Repeat steps two through five until time runs out.

Coaching Points

- Players will get tired quickly; don't let them get lazy and stop doing the little things!

- The outlet must receive the ball below the foul line extended. You'll have one-on-none breaks if you allow them to receive farther up the court.

- Keep score. The losing team runs sprints after the drill is over.

- Out of bounds—give the ball to the team who hustles to get the ball.

Variations

- The time may vary.

- How you keep score may vary. You can give points for things other than a score, for example, an offensive rebound, a good box out, a steal, hustle.

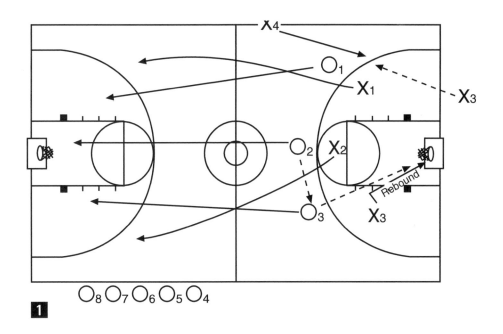

1

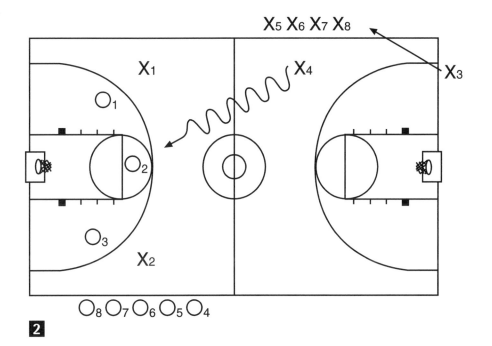

2

Catch Up

Coach Muffet McGraw
School University of Notre Dame

Purpose

To offensively work on a three-on-two situation. To defensively address transition defense.

Organization

Three defenders along the free throw line, three offensive players on the baseline, one ball, three lines.

Procedure

1. The coach throws the ball to any of the three offensive players on the baseline.
2. Whoever has lined up as their defender runs and touches the baseline while the offense takes off three on two.
3. The third defender sprints to catch up, then plays three on three.

Coaching Points

- Defense should form a tandem until the third defender arrives.
- The top player stops the penetration and forces a pass.
- The bottom defender goes out to defend the first pass of the key.
- The last defender down picks up whoever is at the top.

Variation

- Play it out three on three, and come back down court three on three against full-court pressure.

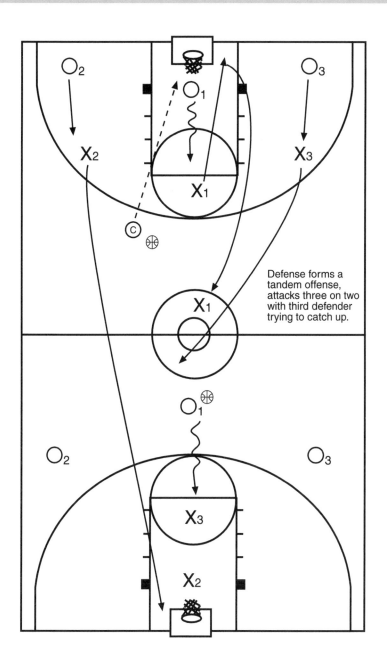

Defense forms a
tandem offense,
attacks three on two
with third defender
trying to catch up.

Three on Three on Three

Coach Tim Shea
School Salem State College

Purpose

To improve communication, to prevent open shots, and to learn to rotate to the open player.

Organization

Players in teams of three with different colored shirts on half a court, one team on offense with the ball, one team on defense. The remaining teams are beneath the basket.

Procedure

1. The team plays three on three until one team scores.

2. The team that gives up the score must leave the court quickly while the next team waiting on the baseline rushes onto the court to identify and locate whom to defend.

3. The scoring team does not wait for the new team to get into good defensive position. They get the ball quickly, clear it behind the 3-point line, pass it in, and play.

4. After a score, only the offensive team may grab the ball.

Coaching Points

- The winning team is the first one to make 10 baskets. If done correctly, the losing teams will be too exhausted for much more than a token penalty sprint.
- Treat a foul the same as a score.
- If two teams have had a few chances on offense, chase them both off the court and bring on the next two teams.
- Your emphasis should be on the team rushing onto the court. Team members need to talk, point, identify perimeter shooters and defend them accordingly.

Variation

- Four on four on four.

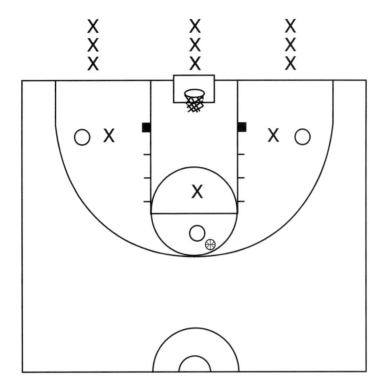

Olympic Drill

Coach Tim Shea
School Salem State College

Purpose

To teach communication, to learn how to play help defense, and to learn how to recover on defense.

Organization

Three offensive players on the end line, facing the coach and three defensive players at the free throw line, facing the offensive players. The coach has the ball at the free throw line. (diagram 1)

Procedure

1. The coach passes the ball to any offensive player on the end line. The three offensive players break down the court.
2. The defender facing the player who received the pass must sprint to and touch the end line while her two teammates are getting back into the paint (see diagram 2).
3. After touching the end line, X_1 must determine where she is most needed while sprinting back.
4. X_2 and X_3 try to force as many passes as possible while protecting the basket and awaiting the help of X_1.
5. Play continues until the offense scores or is stopped.
6. Teams switch (offense to defense) to return down the court to repeat the same setup.

Coaching Points

- The coach may throw the pass to any offensive player.
- Play continues if the offensive team rebounds the ball.
- The coach needs to avoid collision with the ball and players.
- One of the two retreating defenders (X_1) calls, "Ball," while getting back to within 15 feet of the basket. The other defender (X_3) positions herself in the low post area.
- The defenders try to force the offense into making the extra pass, enabling the third defender (X_2) to recover.

Variation

- Allow one of the two retreating defenders to gamble by not going all the way back immediately.

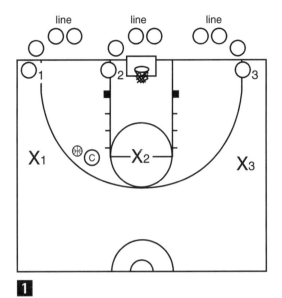

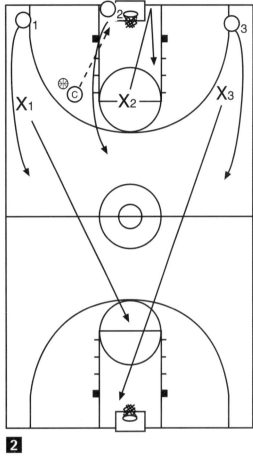

TEAM DRILLS

The Houston Comets' four WNBA titles speak volumes for the concept of team defense. Sure, they have terrific post players and Cynthia Cooper and Sheryl Swoopes, but most of all they have shown repeatedly they can play team defense against anyone!

How does a team of exceptional athletes (or perhaps not so exceptional athletes) excel at such an impressive level? Getting your players to make a defensive commitment and to play intensely without faltering over time is a goal many coaches share, but few have been able to accomplish.

The last section in this book will give you more drills to help put the *team* in your defensive approach. The fundamentals of footwork, rebounding, perimeter and post pressure, screen management, and transition defense will give your players the knowledge and confidence to play against their opponents on any night. What you can do to demand players' focus, attention, and unselfishness may make the same difference that has separated the Houston Comets from the rest of the WNBA.

Three-on-Three Energizer

Coach Kathy Bennett
School Indiana University

Purpose

To emphasize seeing the floor and provide early help and recovery.

Organization

Six players (three offense, three defense) spaced in three lanes, one ball.

Procedure

1. The offense must stay in the lanes and attempt to progress the ball to the other end.
2. The defense tries to keep in front and see the ball at all times.
3. Have the offense try and get the ball past the defense.

Coaching Points

- Off ball, the player must be as low as her player or the ball.
- Show help early; work one-pass help and recovery. When the offensive player gets rid of the ball, move to get in position.
- Don't let the offense get behind the defense. Keep in front to see the ball.

Variation

- Add ball screens when the players cross opposite hash mark and play live three on three, no more lanes.

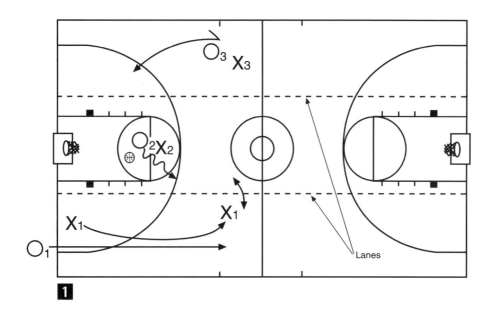

1

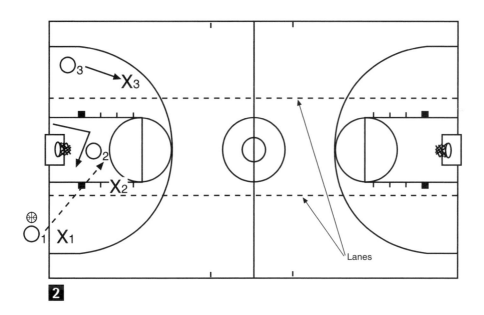

2

Switch Drill

Coach Kathy Bennett
School Indiana University

Purpose
To force the team to talk and communicate. To help with recovering to the correct position, and work on stopping the ball on baseline and middle drives.

Organization
Eight players (four offense and four defense) set in a basic shell alignment, one ball.

Procedure
1. Start in a basic shell (see diagram 1).
2. Offense should try to move any time they can (see diagram 2).
3. When the coach calls the switch, offense sets the ball on the ground.
4. Offense becomes defense in the same shell set, and defense must find a new player to guard. A player cannot guard the person who was previously guarding her (see diagram 3).
5. Try to go for three to five switch calls.

Coaching Points
- Recover to position in relation to the ball.
- Know how to rotate on penetration.
- Communicate.

Variation
- Start in another formation that does not balance the floor.

1

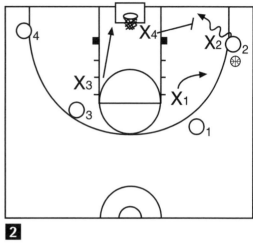

2

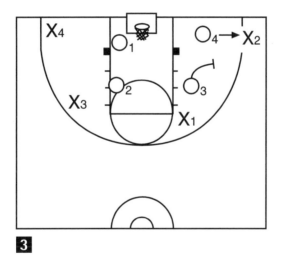

3

Ball Side to Help Side

Coach Kathy Bennett
School Indiana University

Purpose
To teach the importance of ball pressure, rotation on baseline drives, double teaming in the post, recovery out of double teams, and getting from ball side to help side quickly.

Organization
Eight players (four on four), one coach, one ball, half court. Start with the coach or manager on top with the ball unguarded. One post on each block is defended, and the guards at each wing are defended.

Procedure
1. Offense works the ball and tries to get by defense (see diagram 1).
2. When the ball goes inside to the post, try to get effective double teams (see diagram 2).
3. Rotate out of double teams, drive to stop penetration, then recover.

Coaching Points
- If defending the wing guard who passes in to the post, close down and deny ball back out from post.
- Don't let the ball back to anyone but the coach on top (out of the double team).
- Don't let the guard penetrate the middle.

Variation
- Vary the alignments to work four on three.

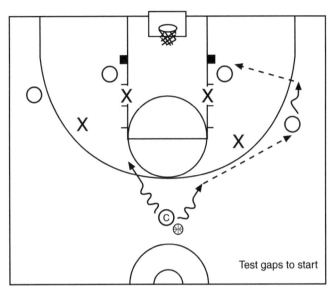

1

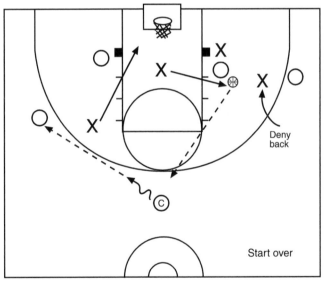

2

Defending Cutters

Coach Nikki Caldwell
School University of Virginia

Purpose

To help players recognize and defend cuts to the ball.

Organization

Six players, offense and defense on the perimeter, two offensive players on the wing and one offensive player inside with defense on each, one ball.

Procedure

1. The ball starts on the wing opposite the player inside. The weak-side defenders on the post and on the wing get to help-side defense (see diagram 1).

2. The weak-side post will cut to the high post.

3. The post defense will step up and cut the cutter in the lane. The post defenders will be denying aggressively.

4. The offensive post player (O_3) will relocate to a ball-side block. Post defense (X_3) will defend that by keeping the offensive player behind her, but staying in a denial stance (see diagram 2).

5. The ball is reversed to the weak-side wing (O_2) by a skip pass. The weak-side defense will go from help side to defending the ball. Make sure X_2 comes out in a stance with her feet moving.

6. The defense (X_1) will have to jump to help-side position. The weak-side wing O_1 will flash to the ball. The help-side defense will defend that cut to the ball. The offensive player will read, go either to the top of the key after the cut or to a ball-side block (see diagram 3).

7. The defender will have to send the offensive player behind her if the cut is made to the block.

Coaching Points

- Cut the cutter and force her away from the basket or behind the defender.
- Don't let the offense cut in front of the defender.
- On the skip pass, the defense will have to get off to the help-side position.

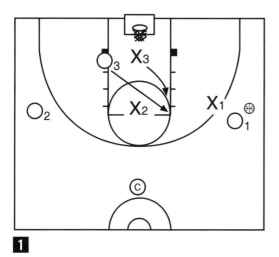

1

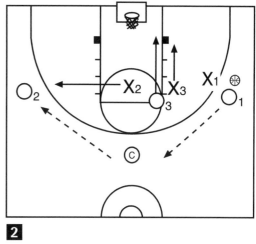

2

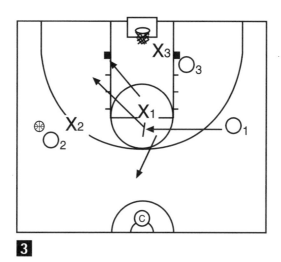

3

Half-Court Converting Drill

Coach Carol Hammerle
School Northern Illinois University

Purpose
To teach players how to defend or stop dribble penetration.

Organization
Four on four, half court.

Procedure
1. Offense can only score in the paint.
2. When coach calls "switch," offense sets the ball down and becomes defense.
3. Players must switch and cannot guard the same person who was guarding them.
4. Defense must sink to the level of the ball and communicate with one another to stop penetration.
5. Defend basket/ball/player, not player/ball/basket.
6. Drill ends with basket made or a defensive stop.

Coaching Points
- Everyone must communicate.
- Everyone must help stop penetration to basket.

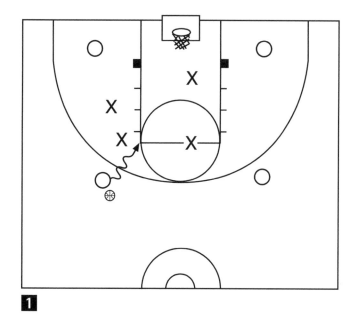

1

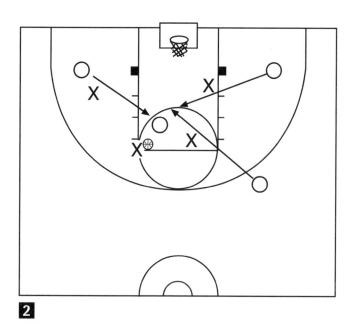

2

Diamond Drill (Four on Five)

Coach Yvonne Kauffman
School Elizabethtown College

Purpose
To practice playing defense when offense outnumbers defense.

Organization
Four defensive players (X), five offensive players (O), one ball.

Procedure
1. Defense sets up in a diamond. Offense sets up point guard, two wings, and two low posts (see diagram 1).
2. Put pressure on the ball. X_2 and X_3 are in denial on the wings; X_4 has two players.
3. Offense passes to the wing. X_1 is now in denial; X_3 is on the ball. X_4 is in denial on the ball-side post; X_2 slips down to split the weak-side post and weak-side wing (see diagram 2).
4. Pass to the post. X_4 is on the ball, and X_3 on ball side plays denial. X_2 slides down and plays denial on the post, and X_1 splits the wing and point guard (see diagrams 3 and 4).

Coaching Points
- To start the drill, offense may not move.
- After defense understands the movement, offense may move.
- Post players may not cut to high post.
- No one may double team.
- Always put pressure on the ball. Denial is one pass away. The player who is two passes away has two players.

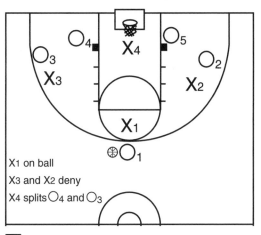

X1 on ball

X3 and X2 deny

X4 splits ○4 and ○3

1

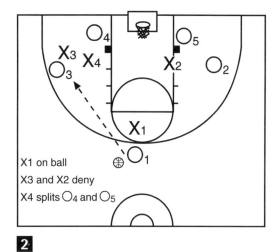

X1 on ball

X3 and X2 deny

X4 splits ○4 and ○5

2

X4 on ball

X2 and X3 deny

X1 splits ○2 and ○1

3

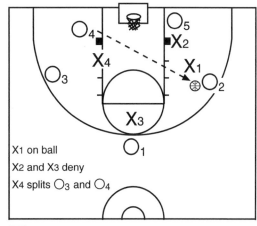

X1 on ball

X2 and X3 deny

X4 splits ○3 and ○4

4

Three Screens (Four on Four)

Coach Andy Landers
School University of Georgia

Purpose

To practice setting and defending three types of screens in a game situation.

Organization

Four offensive, four defensive players, one coach with ball. Players align as offense and defense on the wings and blocks.

Procedure

1. The coach has the ball at the top and starts dribbling to the right. O_1 down screens for O_2 (see diagram 1).
2. O_2 holds for one count, then makes block-to-block screens for O_3 (see diagram 2).
3. After the block-to-block screen takes place, the coach dribbles across the top to the left, then O_1 back screens for O_4.
4. The coach dribbles back to the right, and O_2 starts to down screen.

Coaching Points

- Develop setting good, legal screens.
- Practice defending these screens (the coach decides how to defend them).
- Use the screens effectively; set your player up and make crisp cuts.

Variation

- After everyone goes through all three screens, the coach can pass the ball to someone who is open and play four on four.

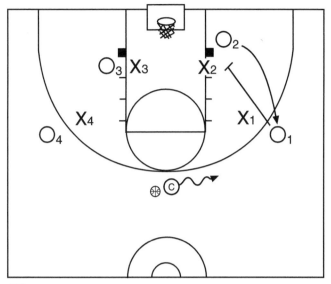

1

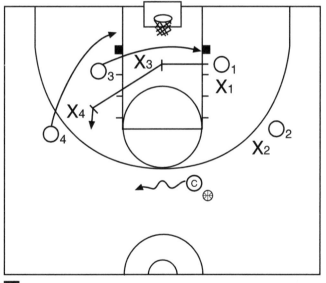

2

Five-on-Five Shell Drill

Coach Wendy Larry
School Old Dominion University

Purpose
To work on perimeter defensive help positioning and communication.

Organization
Ten players (five on offense, five on defense), one ball. Offense should spread out around the perimeter; defense matches up.

Procedure
1. Defense has three positions—on ball, denial, and help. On ball is when your player has the ball, denial is when your player is one pass away, and help is when your player is two or three passes away. The farther your player is from the ball, the farther you can be from your player.
2. The offensive player with the ball makes a pass. The receiver must hold the ball at least three seconds before passing so the defense has the opportunity to get in good position and the coach has an opportunity to make corrections if someone is out of position. Offense must hold the ball and cannot dribble or shoot.
3. Repeat step 2 until you feel the defense knows where they should be and they are getting there. Switch offense and defense.

Coaching Points
- Make sure defense moves on the release of a pass and that they don't stand and watch, then react late.
- Even though this drill is almost slow motion, don't let the defense slack! Make sure they get in *good* position *quickly.* Approach to the ball is important!
- When the offensive player at the top of the key receives the ball, emphasize that if she is in the middle of the court, there is no help! Tell the defender to force her to a side.

Variation
- After your team has gotten good positioning down, you can allow the offense to play live. Give them rules (e.g., only two dribbles, no screens, no shooting until 10 passes are made, no outside shots). This is a positioning drill to teach and review basic concepts.

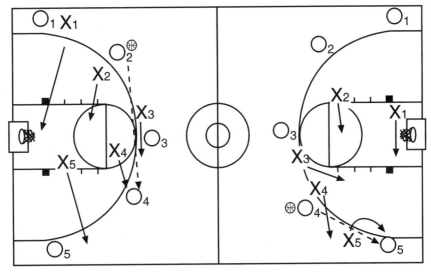

1

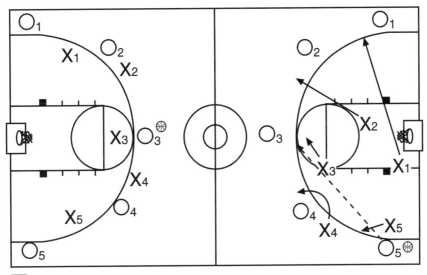

2

Four Out Front (Transition Defense)

Coach Amy Ruley
School North Dakota State University

Purpose

To communicate with teammates in transition, with defense focusing on positioning and player matchups (rotation).

Organization

One ball, four lines at the end line offensive, four defensive players at the free throw line extended facing the end line, two managers as outlets.

Procedure

1. O_4 begins dribbling upcourt, looking to pass ahead to teammates filling respective lanes in fast break.
2. X_4 must sprint and touch the end line before joining teammates in a transition defense.
3. The three other defensive players rotate and match up according to ball position and offensive player movement.
4. The drill is finished when the offensive team scores, or defense creates a turnover or rebounds a missed shot (outlets to the managers on the sideline). Rotation is offense to defense, defense out, and a new set of offensive players comes in from the end line.

Coaching Points

- Stop the ball. The defensive players closest to the ball adjust to the offensive player.
- Communicate. Talk and point to locate the ball while sprinting and backpedaling to match up.
- The offensive team spreads across the floor to challenge defensive spacing.

Variations

- Defense faces the opposite end line and must sprint three hard steps, pivot, and locate the ball.
- Follow fast-break principles or do a patterned break.
- Both offensive and defensive teams circle around the coach, who shoots at the basket. A matchup and rebound outlet sequence fulfills the progression of this drill.

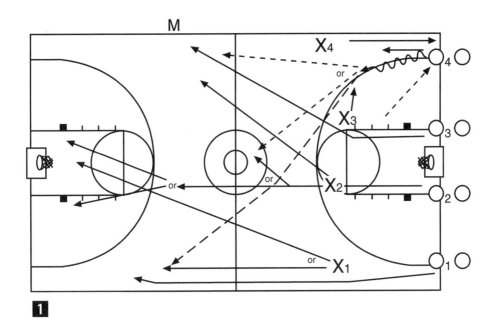

1

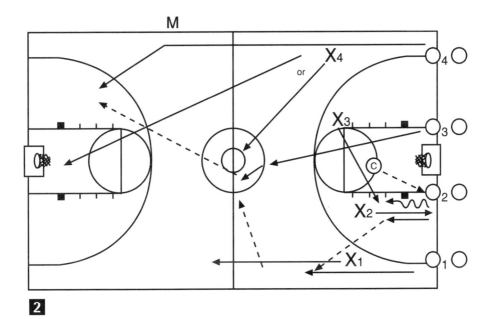

2

Five on Four

Coach Tim Shea
School Salem State College

Purpose
To prevent open shots and rotate to defend open opponents.

Organization
Five offensive players against four defensive players, one ball, half court.

Procedure
1. Offense must make two perimeter passes before shooting or passing inside.
2. The defense always rotates to the ball and does not cover the player farthest from the ball.
3. The ball handler (O_1) is always covered, along with the next two closest offensive players (O_2 and O_3). X_4 watches the remaining two offensive players O_4 and O_5. She will defend whichever one is the most dangerous (see diagram 1).
4. When the ball reaches O_4 (see diagram 2), X_4 *must* drop to defend O_5. X_2 remains on O_2 while X_1 drops into a zonelike position as she awaits movement into a scoring area by either O_1 or O_3.

Coaching Points
- Defense moves to offense when they stop the offense from *scoring* three times *in a row*. Do not consider a foul as stopping the offense. Continue the count.
- Don't allow the four defenders to play a zone. They must cover someone. Only one defender is in a zonelike position at any one time.
- Never give up a good shot to anyone! If you must, leave your player and defend the open player.

Variation
- Four on three.

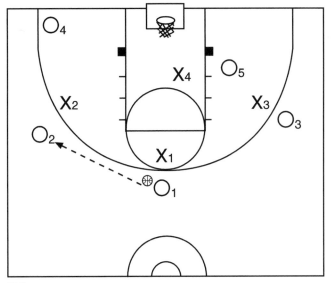

1

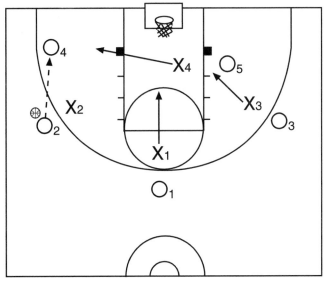

2

Three-on-Three Continuous Motion Drill

Coach Dave Smith
School Bellarmine College

Purpose

To teach defensive players how to defend each type of screen or cut. In this continuous drill, players will have to defend a down screen, back screen, cross screen, pick and roll, shuffle cut, pick the picker situation, and deny cutters.

Organization

Six players (three on offense and three on defense), one coach, one ball. You may station additional players off the court and ready to rotate in.

Procedure

1. Begin the drill with O_1 in the point position, O_3 in the high post, and O_2 at the low block. Defense matches up accordingly.
2. The drill begins with a down screen, then flows continuously to the shuffle cut, pick and roll, deny cutters, back screen, deny high post cutter, cross screen, pick the picker. The coach is off to the side of the court the drill begins on (see diagrams 1-8).
3. When the teams have completed the sequence of defensive situations, the offensive players leave the court, the defensive players become the offense, and three new defensive players come on the court.

Coaching Points

- Emphasize communication, such as calling out screens, ball, shot, and so on, the little things you want your players to do on defense.
- You may prefer to defend some situations differently; simply adjust how the players defend each situation according to your defensive philosophy.
- In the beginning we are trying to teach defensive techniques and how we want to defend each situation. When we are confident that our players understand and can execute each defensive strategy, then we begin to play the drill live.

Variation

- In teaching, you can make each situation a two-on-two drill, with the coach becoming a passer or receiver as necessary, before going to the full sequence of situations.

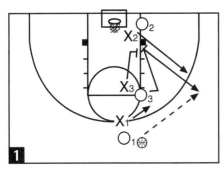

1

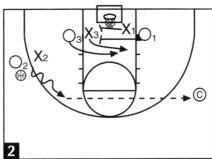

2

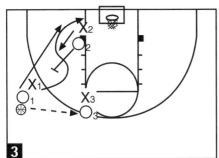

3

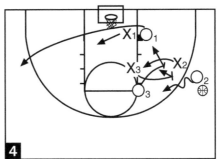

4

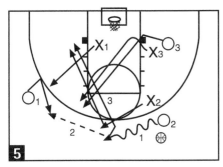

5

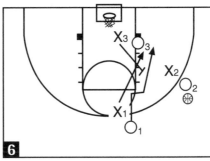

6

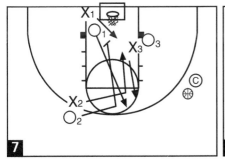

7

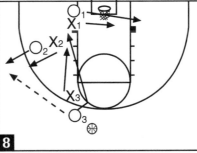

8

1 O_3 sets a downscreen for O_2; X_2 follows around the screen; X_3 hedges to defend the curl; O_2 cuts to the wing.

2 O_2 dribbles the ball for reversal and passes to O_1; O_2 then makes a basket cut; X_2 jumps to the ball on the pass and them makes O_2 cut behind him; O_3 then cuts from the weakside low to the ballside high post; X_3 repositions on pass to O_2 and denies O_3 through the lane; O_1 passes to O_2.

3 O_2 dribbles for reversal and passes the ball to the coach or manager; O_1 cross screens for O_3; X_1 takes away baseline cut from O_3; X_3 fights over the top of the screen and denies O_3 across the lane.

4 As O_1 passes to O_2, O_3 sets up a backscreen for O_1 at the elbow; O_1 shuffle cuts off the screen; X_3 hedges to help on the cutter; X_1 pivots and goes under the screen to catch back up with O_1.

5 O_1 passes to O_2; O_2 sets a backscreen for O_1; X_2 calls the screen and gives X_1 room to slide through; X_1 pivots and slides over the top of the screen then goes through to the cutter.

6 After O_3 cuts off the cross screen; O_2 sets a pick for the picker O_1; here X_2 calls the switch with X_1; X_2 denies cutter O_1 and X_1 steps ballside of O_2.

7 O_3 then sets a pick on the ball for O_2; O_2 and O_3 execute a pick and roll; X_1 moves to a helpside position; X_3 steps on top of the screen to hedge and rolls with O_3 to defend the pick and roll; O_2 pivots and goes under the screen to catch back up with and stop a drive to the basket.

8 O_2 steps out after the backscreen; O_3 passes to O_2; O_1 continues backdoor cut to the weak side; O_3 V-cuts and makes a basket cut; X_2 closes on O_2; X_1 moves to help position; X_3 jumps to the ball and makes O_3's cut behind.

Three-on-Three Half-Court Defensive Drill

Coach Nancy Winstel
School Northern Kentucky University

Purpose

To teach proper defensive positioning, on the ball, one pass away (denial), and help side. To teach defensively how to defend ball screens and screens away from the ball. This drill also helps players learn how to make a strong cut, how to set and use screens, and how to find the open person.

Organization

Players are separated into groups of three at half court—three on offense, three on defense. Other groups of three are out, ready to substitute in (you can have groups of four with one substitute also). Players rotate offense to defense, defense out.

Procedure

1. The drill begins at half court with the offensive players working on keeping the ball alive, setting good ball screens, using the screens, and making good cuts.

2. The defense concentrates on putting good pressure on the ball (forcing the ball to the sideline) and being active. If the ball is picked up, defense is in full-pressure defense. If a ball screen occurs, have the defense move toward their players and go over top of the screen. Allow players to switch (see diagrams 1-4).

Coaching Points

- The coach will stop the drill throughout and make sure that players are talking (calling out screens, calling out help).

Variations

- Run this drill initially at the half-court area facing the basket, without taking any shots. Focus on pressuring the ball, pressuring the passing lanes, defending screens on and off the ball, and playing good help defense.

- Have the defense play until they get a steal or until the 30-second clock expires.

- Allow offensive players to shoot, drive and post.

- Have the players switch on all screens. Defense steps out when switching, pressuring the ball hard.

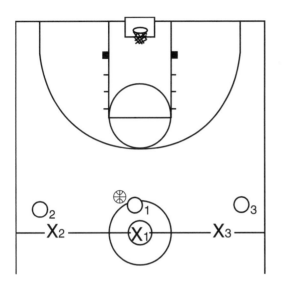

1

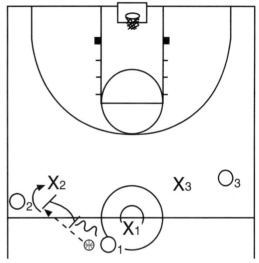

2

O₁ screens away,
giving a lane for O₃.

3

O₁ options:
1. Cut to basket
2. Screen on ball
3. Screen away
Defense must defend accordingly.

4

Coach Nancy Winstel
School Northern Kentucky University

Purpose

To teach proper defensive positioning in the post; to teach movement, intensity, communication with teammates, concentration, hand-eye coordination, and working in a situation where there is confusion.

Organization

Ten players and two coaches. Three of the ten are on offense and three on defense set in a triangle (these players are actively involved in the drill). The other four players are passers on the perimeter. There is one ball on the perimeter that the four perimeter players pass. There are two coaches on the court, and they each have a ball.

Procedure

1. The drill begins with everyone in position (see diagram 1).

2. The offensive players inside stay in their positions and don't move much. The defensive post players do all the work.

3. The perimeter players pass the ball to one another throughout the drill; they may skip pass or make a direct pass. This ball determines the position that the defense plays in relationship to their offensive players. This ball is *never* passed inside. The balls that the coaches have get passed inside, one ball at a time, and only when the perimeter ball is on that side. The defense moves quickly, retrieves the ball, and immediately returns the ball to the coach. The drill moves fast, balls are flying, and players are moving (see diagram 2).

4. The drill is complete when the players have played defense at all three spots.

Coaching Points

- The coach keeps the drill active by having the perimeter players move the ball quickly.
- The defense must talk and move throughout the drill.
- The coaches make all types of passes: chest, bounce, lobs, roll the ball, etc., while constantly checking to make sure the defense is in proper position.

Variation

- As the ball is moving along the perimeter, the coach can call "shot," and the defensive players must turn and box.

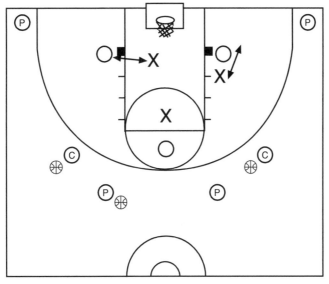

1

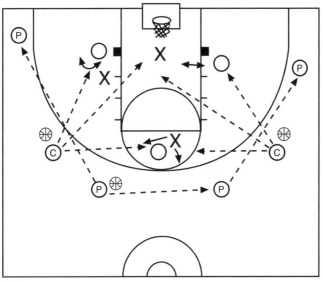

2

Triangle Rebounding (Perimeter Series)

Coach Nancy Winstel
School Northern Kentucky University

Purpose

To teach proper box out techniques; defensive positioning techniques for perimeter players and the fundamentals of the fast break.

Organization

Two coaches; three players in each group, four to five groups, or three groups of four (only three players in at a time). Two balls, one for the drill and one out of the drill, are ready to go immediately at the completion of the drill.

Procedure

1. Three offensive and three defensive players set up in a triangle begin the drill. The coaches pass the ball to one another and also to defensive players who are in proper defensive position if so inlined.

2. Coaches may also dribble with penetration to have the defense stop the ball.

3. After moving the ball quickly back and forth, a coach shoots, and the defensive players go to their offensive players, make good contact on the box out, and get the ball. After a defender secures the rebound, she outlets the ball to a teammate. The play continues with the defenders filling their lanes as they run to half court. Meanwhile, the first offensive team goes to defense, and three new players come in on offense. The drill moves quickly.

Coaching Points

- The coaches move the drill quickly and demand intensity from players. Make sure that players make contact on all box outs.

- If the shot is made and offense gets the rebound, play three on three until the goal is made or until the defense secures a rebound. If offense makes a basket, defense quickly inbounds the ball and looks for a transition.

Variations

- The coach passes to a wing offensive player; the player beats her defender to the baseline. Defense calls for help, and help stops the ball. The top slides down, and the player who got beat slides up to box out of offense. The player who drove the baseline takes a jump shot (see diagram 3).

- This time offense keeps the drive, and help must take charge. Everyone else on defense must rotate and box out an offensive player (see diagram 4).

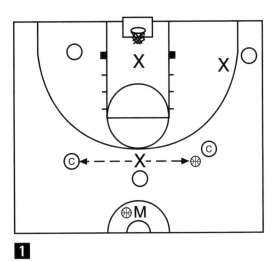

1

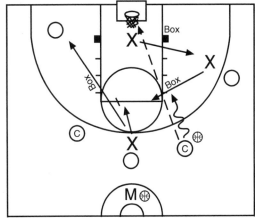

2

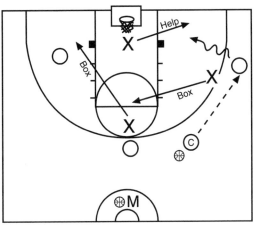

3

4

Triangle Rebounding (Post Series)

Coach Nancy Winstel
School Northern Kentucky University

Purpose

To teach proper rebounding box out techniques, proper post-defensive positioning, communication, intensity, and the beginning of the fast break.

Organization

Three players in each group, four or five groups, or three groups of four (only three in at a time). Two balls, one for drill and one out of the drill, are ready to go immediately at the completion of the drill.

Procedure

1. Players begin the drill with three on offense and three on defense in a triangle in the post area (see diagram 1). There are two passers on the baseline and no defense.

2. One coach has the ball. The coaches pass the ball to one another, checking proper defensive positioning throughout the drill. The coaches can dribble to make defense react.

3. After a few passes, one coach shoots the ball. The players must make contact on the box, and then go get the rebound. After the defense controls the rebound, an outlet is made to a teammate and the break begins. Meanwhile, the first offensive team goes to defense and three new players come in on offense. The drill moves quickly.

Coaching Points

- The coaches move the drill quickly, demanding intensity from the players. Make players be physical in this drill.

- If the shot is made and offense gets the rebound, play three on three until the goal is made or until defense secures a rebound. If a player makes a basket, quickly inbound the ball.

Variations

- The coach passes to the wing. She passes to the post player on the block who has beaten her player. The defense must rotate to pick up and box out the shooter and the other offensive players (see diagram 3). In diagram 4 we use the same drill, but now the help defense must step in and take the charge. The other two defenders rotate and box out.

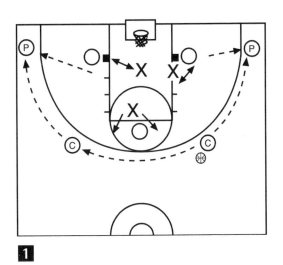

1

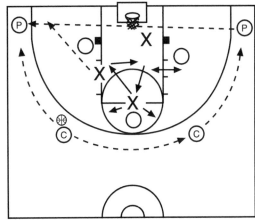

take charge

2

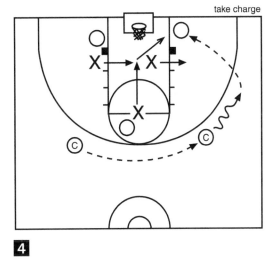

3

4

ABOUT THE WBCA

Founded in 1981, the Women's Basketball Coaches Association (WBCA) is the largest such organization in the United States. Its mission is to promote women's basketball by unifying coaches at all levels to develop a reputable identity for the sport of women's basketball and to foster and promote the development of the game in all of its aspects as an amateur sport for women and girls.

The WBCA is involved in several events and clinics throughout the year, including: the High School All-America Game (televised on ESPN2), the three-day educational Coaches' Academy, WBCA Premier Basketball Camps, the WBCA All-Star Challenge, the Coaches vs. Cancer Challenge, coaching clinics across the nation, and Sears Collegiate Champions (SCC) program. Through these events the WBCA not only tries to highlight exceptional talent among women and girl players but also provides opportunities for coaches at all levels to better themselves.

In addition to the activities that the WBCA puts on and sponsors, they have an extensive awards program through which the best, brightest, and most talented athletes, coaches, and contributors to women's basketball are honored. There is also the annual WBCA National Convention held in conjunction with the NCAA Women's Final Four and their three publications (*Coaching Women's Basketball, At the Buzzer,* and *Fastbreak Alert*), which provide coverage on all aspects of women's basketball from high school to professional.

For more details on these and the many activities and opportunities available from the WBCA, check out their Web site at: **www.wbca.org**.

The following are coaches who contributed drills to *WBCA's Defensive Basketball Drills*:

- Jane Albright, University of Wisconsin
- Cindy Anderson, Loyola College
- Ceal Barry University of Colorado
- Kathy Bennett, Indiana University
- Gary Blair, University of Arkansas
- Lisa Bluder, Drake University
- Beth Burns, Ohio State University
- Nikki Caldwell, University of Virginia
- Marnie Daiko, Cornell University
- Elaine Elliott, University of Utah
- Nancy Fahey, Washington University
- Theresa Grentz, University of Illinois
- Carol Hammerle, Northern Illinois University
- Bonnie Henrickson, Virginia Tech
- Kris Huffman, Depaw University
- Yvonne Kauffman, Elizabethtown College
- Andy Landers, University of Georgia
- Wendy Larry, Old Dominion University
- Muffet McGraw, University of Notre Dame
- June Olkowski, Northwestern University
- Jody Rajcula, Western Connecticut State University
- Amy Ruley, University of North Dakota
- Jody Runge, University of Oregon
- Tim Shea, Salem College
- Dave Smith, Bellarmine College
- Pat Summit, University of Tennessee
- Nancy Winstel, Northern Kentucky University
- Kay Yow, North Carolina State University

Excel on the offensive end, too!

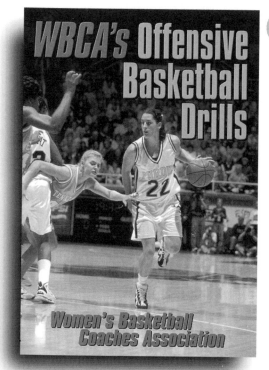